REMARRIAGE
In the Middle Years and Beyond

Phyllis S. Kamm

prises
nia

Printed in the United States of America.

ISBN 1-55867-027-0
Library of Congress Catalog Card No. 91-075891

Cover design by Frank Paredes

DEDICATION

This book is dedicated to Herb, my husband, companion and professional mentor for the more than 54 years of our marriage. As any good editor should (and he's the best), he has been my toughest critic and strongest supporter.

I am grateful for his editorial expertise and his good-humored acceptance of all that dining out during the months spent writing *Remarriage*.

His professional and constant loving support have always been appreciated but, in this instance, it was invaluable.

Acknowledgments

Many thanks to:

Arthur Bourdon, Jr., C.P.A, for expert guidance through the complexities of financial and tax information that become more and more confusing with each new equation introduced.

And to David C. Fitzpatrick, attorney-at-law, for his legal expertise about pre- and postnuptial contracts and all the ramifications involved in the legal aspects of a remarried family.

Their professional help and friendship have been inestimable. However, I absolve Arthur and David from responsibility for any legal or technical errors I may have made while trying to translate all their data into readable, understandable text.

CONTENTS

REMARRIAGE: FOR THE MIDDLE YEARS AND BEYOND

This book, considered a guide to a major life decision, is an outgrowth of five years of researching, interviewing and coauthoring a book about grief and bereavement, *About Mourning, Support and Guidance for the Bereaved,* which was published in 1985 by Human Sciences Press, New York.

It was inevitable that some of the men and women to whom I talked would have been widowed and remarried and that their experiences and feelings about remarriage would emerge during those interviews.

It also was not unusual that during all those years of preparation for the book about mourning, I collected reams of notes about remarriage from books and articles by sources as divergent as Freud, Jung, Margaret Meade, Gail Sheehy, *The New York Times, Dear Abby* and many other experts and nonexperts on family relations.

Remarriage is often the next hoped-for stage of a person's life after the loss of a mate whether because of divorce or death. Many who fulfill that hope are ready for it; some walk down the aisle blindly, unready and perhaps even unfit to deal with the vicissitudes of the new relationship.

I hope this book will help prepare mature men and women contemplating remarriage to face the dilemmas that inevitably will arise. I hope it will guide them toward an intelligent decision about their future.

The book on bereavement was, of course, a serious examination of a unique time in the life of an individual and family.

Although this book on remarriage also is serious and about another unique time that affects individuals and their families, it is not solemn. I make no pretense about it being a profound scientific, psychological and sociological epic.

Nevertheless, as a journalist, I have learned to study and analyze a situation and to present a lucid, cogent report.

Anthony Pietropinto, M.D., and Jacqueline Simenauer point out in *Husbands and Wives, a Nationwide Survey of Marriage*, that psychotherapists and marriage counselors themselves have a high divorce rate. That does not necessarily negate their clinical abilities. But they concede that someone needing marriage counseling "might well react upon learning of the therapist's personal track record as though he had unwittingly enrolled in the Don Rickles charm school or the Phyllis Diller beauty program."

Despite Pietropinto's and Simenauer's candor, I am grateful to all the psychologists, family counselors, sociologists, philosophers and those in my own profession whose studies and writings were helpful. They eased both my original research for the bereavement book and the additional search for enlightenment on the subjects of remarriage, family relationships and stepparenting in preparation for this book.

The authors of *Husbands and Wives* went on to say: "The problem is that we hear far too little from people currently involved in marriages — not ideal marriages, not extraordinary unions and exceptional partnerships, but ordinary, functional relationships which somehow manage to survive the pressures of environment, family, mate and one's own person."

The statement confirms my belief that "ordinary" people must be involved in an examination of any life situation before there can evolve an intelligent guide for coping with the inevitable questions.

So I also am grateful to those who sat for personal interviews for the bereavement book and for this one, as well as the persons who completed special questionnaires for this latest study.

(An interesting sidelight is that almost all of the women polled completed and returned the questionnaires, sometimes with valuable candor. Of the married couples, however, only half of the men returned them at all. Of those who did, most of the answers were succinct, with little elaboration of feelings.)

The persons who participated in this study were selected in a totally unscientific, random manner. However, even though there are variations in the situations, emotions and coping mechanisms, my data were confirmed and reinforced by the information gleaned from studies and writings of numerous professionals in the field.

When you boil it all down, professionals and non-professionals — psychologists, psychiatrists, family counselors and advice-to-the-confused columnists — tend to give basically the same recommendations for confronting the complexities that arise and decisions that must be made before and after a remarriage. A number of publications now on the market tend to deal with only one or two phases of the reconstituted family.

I have tried to develop an integrated theme that covers different remarriage situations. Although each has its own quandaries, there are threads of similarity that weave through second marriages for older couples with adult children or no children, and younger couples with or without children.

This book concentrates primarily on remarriage among the middle-aged and older generations. All of the cases cited are true stories about real people. Only the names have been changed to protect the privacy of the individuals.

Even though remarriage is a highly significant life event, that does not mean a guide to remarriage should be a doleful tome. I have sprinkled bits of levity amid the serious discussions about coping with the perplexities to encourage men and women who are considering this important step to keep their funnybones tingling. Maintaining one's sense of humor should enhance the value of the ideas offered in these pages, rather than diminish them.

I hope this book will help you choose wisely. But even when your choice is less than perfect, adjustments can be made through thoughtfulness and cooperative effort.

CHAPTER 1: HOW GOOD ARE THE POSSIBILITIES FOR REMARRIAGE?

Historian-philosopher Bertrand Russell was merely reporting the history of human mating when he wrote: "Man is not a solitary animal."

Since Biblical times (and probably before), men and women have sought the comfort and companionship of the opposite sex. If, for one reason or another, the first mate disappeared, there were often new alliances. So remarriage, or whatever it was called in the particular milieu, has been an integral part of the fabric of many cultures since time immemorial.

Perhaps the methods of choosing mates — first, second and even third — were different in other eras, but today's mating games are played out in numerous arenas and under many circumstances much different from the selection processes of the past. I doubt if anyone in western cultures now follows the Biblical injunction that a man marry his brother's widow; nor does a father choose his daughter's bridegroom.

Maybe empire and politics still have a role in some instances (the few surviving monarchies, for example), but even that idea is being relegated to history. Today everyone is left to one's own devices to find a mate.

Sometimes a person plunges impetuously into a new liaison because of romantic dreams, plain old sexual attraction, cold-blooded social climbing or because one is seeking financial security.

It is the nature of man that there comes a time after widowhood or divorce when some women and men want to reach out from the solitude of singleness. At that point they may be ready for remarriage and the gods smile on them.

The lucky ones

Molly (30 when she remarried): "At first I thought I'd never love anyone the way I loved Jim so I would never remarry ... but when I began to feel again I knew I'd find someone to love me and marry me."

Steve (68): "I never thought at my advanced age I would find a renewal like this with Edith. You live again instead of existing. When you begin to fall in love again, you start to live again."

Doris (65): "I was firmly convinced I would never remarry, but I never figured on my little friend."

Bert (75): "Ruth and I were married with a wedding party consisting of 25 siblings ... Neither of us can believe that, after so much love with our first spouses, we could find such love again."

The unlucky ones

If you are a candidate for remarriage, you are not unique. Many people remarry — not always happily.

Emma (55 when she remarried): "I fell like a ton of bricks — like a schoolgirl. I thought of nothing but 'This is a great guy.' I knew he was a manic-depressive, but when you fall in love you lose all perspective." The marriage ended in divorce after a lot of anger and grief.

Ina (68): "I love him," she told his daughter. She literally closed her eyes to his moodiness when she said, "I do." Two years later, her patience exhausted, she walked out on him.

Are the odds with you or against you?

There are three categories of "solitary animals" in the adult female population. They are widows, divorcees and the never-marrieds whether by design or chance.

The 1990 census indicates there are 11.5 million widows, most of them between the ages of 30 and 70, with a median age of 56. Fifty percent of all women over 65 are widows. A recent study indicated that nearly 85% of all married women eventually will be widows and probably will survive 16 years beyond the original widowhood.

The sequence of marriage, divorce, remarriage is a phenomenon of our culture. With the staggering statistics of 50% of all marriages ending in divorce, more than half a million women re-enter the marriage market each year. About 10% of them are over the age of 60.

Of all persons between the ages of 45 and 64 who remarry, 21.9% are men. Of that group, 20.1% were previously divorced.

On the October 19, 1990 television show *20/20*, in a segment about *Divorce After 60*, Hugh Downs, co-host of the show, reported that "most older break-ups are initiated by the husbands."

Comments on the same program indicated that many of those late divorces were because the older men frequently sought marriage to younger women in a desperate effort to grab at the youth they felt slipping away.

However, in their book, *The Divorce Experience*, Morton and Bernice Hunt dismissed the middle-aged divorced man/young woman marriage as a myth. My own research supports that wisdom. Most men over 60 seek companionship and remarriage with women of their own generation.

When it comes to divorce, the odds are no more encouraging for women now than they were in the 1970s and 1980s.

Of all persons between 45 and 64 who remarry, only 14.9% are women; 2.8% of those were previously divorced.

For women over 65 the statistics offer even less hope for remarriage. That group represents only 2.8% of all remarriages; 0.7% were previously divorced.

The median age at remarriage for divorced men is the mid-30s, but among widowed men it is close to 63. Widowed women remarry at a median age of 54; median age for divorced women is 33.

Add to these statistics about widowed or divorced women the uncounted numbers of never-marrieds and the odds against remarriage become awesome.

It might be tempting for a woman to jump at the first proposal because she's frightened by the hard fact of life — that unmarried women in the United States outnumber unmarried men by a ratio of 4 to 1.

Nevertheless, the merry-go-round continues as more a part of our lives than ever before. That may be why so many single women plunge in impetuously — if not blindly — without facing some hard realities and seeking answers to some tough questions.

The realities include the fact that one good marriage (ended by the death of the loved one) does not necessarily beget another; and one troubled marriage ended by divorce needn't mean problems the second time around.

Therefore, it would be prudent and pragmatic to confront such tough questions as:

- Are you marrying for love or money — or both?
- Are your children exerting too much influence on your decision — one way or the other?

- Will clashing careers lead to marital clashes?
- Do you really love the person or are you responding to your sexual needs?
- Are you completely certain about your motives?

Don't let the statistics scare you into a bad decision.

Despite the wisdom of historian Russell, circumstances leave many women struggling and losing the battle to become part of what anthropologist Margaret Mead, more than 40 years ago, referred to as "the toughest institution we have — the family."

They are reaching for the gold ring but finding that prize elusive.

There have been many changes in the mores and economics of American life in the years since the two scholars, Russell and Mead, put forth their ideas. There also has been that dramatic increase in the disparity between the numbers of single men and single women. This evolution has made it *more difficult for women* to find a mate.

When you think about the statistics, you must admit the odds are not encouraging. So, out of fear of not finding a new spouse, some women rush to the altar at the first opportunity without due consideration. After the bloom of passion — or other motivating force — fades, there may be regrets.

(And although men have a rich field of available women to choose from, they, too, may remarry impetuously, with their emotions and not their heads.)

Therefore, one ought to consider (among other things) that the re-divorce rate is *double* that of first marriage divorces. And the possibility of another unhappy union can increase with each successive divorce.

Even if you beat the odds, win a proposal and are planning to accept the invitation to your own wedding, don't be dazzled by the prospect of wedded bliss — or a new meal ticket.

If wedded bliss is what you're seeking, first try to disentangle reality from emotions and see if there is a foundation for the happy and stable relationship you want for the rest of your life.

One of the major stumbling blocks can be an uncompleted mourning process. And that is pertinent whether the mourning is for the death of a beloved mate or the loss of a particular part of your life through divorce.

Maggie Scarf wrote in *Unfinished Business*: "Unless a person accepts and flows with the transition from one stage of life to another, she or he can become the victim of too many unfinished tasks — too much bitterness, anxiety and stagnation."

It is of primary importance that the mourning process be completed to eliminate any residue of negative emotions that might interfere with the new relationship.

So you've beaten the odds. Now what?

Okay. You've won the toss of the dice. You are planning to say "yes." Don't walk in with blinders limiting your vision of the future. There's a better way to reach a decision.

The following chapters offer ideas and stimulate creative thinking. The result should be a good base for a happy relationship for the rest of your life.

CHAPTER 2 CONSIDER REMARRIAGE

A gift from the gods? Take a good look.

As a candidate for remarriage, you are not unique. Many people get married a second — or a third or fourth — time. But, in a sense, you are unique. It is *your* life, *your* happiness that are on the line. Some imaginative thinking before you say "I do" can lead to the best resolution.

The opportunity to remarry may seem like a gift to be quickly embraced, but sometimes emotion and eagerness influence a choice that should be reached through thoughtful process. You should be prepared to face the issue with intelligence and foresight and not exclusively as a need to fulfill the emotional void in your life. Understanding yourself, your motives and your first marriage may be far more important than sexual attraction.

That is a lot easier preached than practiced. It's especially true when an older person is lonely, a younger one with children is temporarily overwhelmed by the problems of single parenting, or marriage appears to be a safe haven from financial worries.

Does a previous marriage help?

Added to those misguided reasons may be the

belief that one's previous marriage was preparation for a second one. Studies show that great differences in the pace of maturation, life experiences and, yes, age, often contribute to the marital discord that ends in divorce.

So don't kid yourself. Last year's classroom was different from today's. But don't close the door on the idea because it most often does work out — experience and maturity do help.

Bill said: "I had a successful first marriage and wanted a stable life with a stable person who had no other personal commitment."

When Doris, a 62-year-old widow, was contemplating remarriage, she thought: "If one has been married before, it should be easier because one has been over the ground once before."

Too often overlooked is that different personality, character and life experiences make the prospective new mate a totally new figure. The answer will not be the same as last time. Thus, approaching the situation with the old equation in mind could lead to the wrong answer.

While it is true that *middle-aged and older persons* who had successful first marriages usually have compatible second marriages, the simple fact of a satisfactory previous marriage is not a free ticket to a good one the next time. In fact, it emphasizes the need for an intellectual as well as emotional approach to the prospect.

Love can be a sad delusion.

Be wary of a marriage founded on high marks for your first marriage, or on an emotional decision based on loneliness, a response to kindness, or as is more likely among younger persons, on sexual attraction. It rests on a shaky foundation. Understanding yourself and your motives is an ingredient for building a solid base for marriage.

That does not mean one can disregard emotion or passion. A satisfying sexual relationship is a positive element that contributes to the well-being of each of the pair. Both emotion and passion — a good sexual relationship — are essential for a good marriage. But they are only part of the formula. There must also be a mutual commitment to making the union a strong and friendly relationship, too.

A decision for remarriage is not one to be made while lolling in a bubble bath and daydreaming about last night's amour. The prospect must be approached with pragmatism as well as passion.

When Doris talked about loneliness, she admitted: "I had more or less come to terms with it and was almost reluctant to give up my freedom. But the need to share my hopes, failures, dreams, sorrows and joys with someone I loved proved to be stronger than the need to be me."

Although she recommended remarriage before five years pass because one tends to become set in behavioral patterns, there really is no specific time limit. It depends on the individual's ability and willingness to face problems, articulate them and cooperate in making adjustments.

Ina was a widow for 20 years before her remarriage. Even though hers ended unhappily, there are marriages after a long period of singleness that do work out well.

The imminent prospect of remarriage may elicit unrealistic expectations and fears that those expectations will not become reality. Don't set your sights so high the ends will be unattainable. But don't set them too low, either.

The realities and emotions have to be weighed. And it might help to take a look at why some marriages fail.

A large number of divorces — especially in the later years — occur because of increasing differences in the intellectual and social growth of the parties. Different life experiences may contribute to marital discord and failure. Those differences could be because she is too dedicated to home and children to keep her mind stimulated; her spouse too occupied with his career. Or it might be that he resents her successful career while he believes his is stalemated. A third possibility is that one or the other continues to develop and nurture new interests while the other thinks retirement is meant for nothing more stimulating than daytime television or playing golf with the guys.

Other possible causes for disenchantment and divorce: either husband or wife may have an ego so big that it overpowers the marital relationship and upsets the harmony of the marriage.

Or there may be confusion and unhappiness because one partner has a fixed idea of the roll of each one in marriage. Even in the 1990s, there are men who think wives should be homebodies rather than out in the marketplace. Or, if they concede the right of their wives to work, there are objections to a real career — even one already established. It's okay, this kind of logic goes, for a wife to be a part time saleslady in a boutique or department store, but forget about being an executive.

A woman needs a strong sense of her own identity and that is difficult with a narrow-minded or managing mate.

Still other problems identified by marriage counselors are money management, sexual incompatibility, difficulties with children, use of leisure time, in-law relationships, division of household and family responsibilities.

If you believe you're in love, give yourself time to think about your love. *Not passions, love* — that emotion one speaks of too lightly and which often is really only an emphemeral response to physical attraction, kindness or loneliness.

The eminent psychotherapist, Erich Fromm, cautioned about misjudging a response to loneliness that leads one to think it is love. "There is hardly any activity, any enterprise, which is started with such tremendous hopes and expectations, and yet, which fails so regularly as love."

A good marriage is based on love that encompasses respect, understanding, kindness, compassion and communication as well as sexual response.

Love implies, according to Fromm, " a reaction to unexpressed needs between two people." An important factor in love is respecting and trying to understand the other person's self; accepting each other even when there are certain unacceptable habits or behavior patterns; accepting that your partner's ideas and needs do not always coincide with your own.

Without the combination of consideration, understanding, compromise and sixth sense to respond to those "unexpressed needs," there is little ability to adjust to the other person's foibles and to be open and flexible when things go awry. Sometimes one mistakes one's own intransigence for conviction; the difference is between rockbound stubbornness and principle. Carl Jung points out that "Conviction easily turns to self defense and is seduced into rigidity and this is inimical to life." The test of a firm conviction is its flexibility — which means being able to admit error and go on from there without anger or recrimination.

And don't think just because you're charmed by his gentlemanliness — or her caretaking skills — that's all you need to know about your possible intended. Choosing a mate because of an acceptable "personality package," as Fromm labels certain social characteristics, is not the wisest criterion. The reasons for considering remarrying ought to be scrutinized before a decision is made.

There are guidelines for developing skills to make a new marriage work. There is a process that may help a person in the direction of an intelligent decision. It begins with an honest analysis of one's self, one's motives, and the relationship between the man and woman. It will lead to a wiser choice about how to spend the rest of your life.

Briefly, the process entails certain steps. They will be expanded on in subsequent chapters.

1. Put the past in perspective.
2. Lay a good foundation — three watchwords: *Communication, Negotiation, Compromise.*
3. Engage in self-analysis: take a good look at yourself and plan for the future.
4. Involve your future mate in analysis and plans.
5. Consider the health of both parties.
6. Look at your religious beliefs — intermarriage.
7. Discuss and arrange your finances; prenuptial contracts, wills, etc.
8. Bring the children (regardless of age) into the process — the remarried family.
9. Plan the wedding.

Are your reasons for choosing remarriage good ones?

We know there are more opportunities for men to remarry than for women.

We also know the odds favor younger women more than their older compatriots. Young women must confront certain dilemmas.

But the widowed or divorced parents of those younger women are confronted by their own dilemmas. This book attempts to answer some of the questions facing the generations over 50.

Regardless of sex, age, length of previous marriage, whether there are teenaged or adult children, or no children, a person should be careful not to remarry because "The children need a mother (or father)," because "I can't manage the responsibilities," because "I'm terribly lonely," or because the children are fond of the man or woman being dated. Nor, as discussed earlier, should the decision be based on what might be only a temporary emotional involvement.

There are good reasons for remarriage, but it is prudent to examine each facet of the situation before the final vows are spoken.

CHAPTER 3 THE PROCESS: THE FIRST STEPS

Put the past in perspective.

First, one must put the past in proper perspective and face the future with an open and creative mind. That does not mean trying to wipe your mind clean of the past — an impossible task. It means de-emphasizing it, using and profiting from lessons learned — the good things done, the mistakes made — to build a solid foundation for a new marriage.

It is natural to remember a previous mate and the relationship, whether it was ended by death or divorce. It is unnatural to try to obliterate memories of that part of your history.

"Do I think of Buck?" Doris didn't have to ponder the question even though she and Bob had been married more than a year. "Not a day goes by that I don't think of him in some context or other ... I've accepted the fact that he is dead and I'll never see him again. Yet with this acceptance there is a deep sadness, for I miss him and his ribald sense of humor. Another thing I miss is that magnificent, logical mind of his. How I admired this in him ... things he used to say and do ... even though there were times I could have scalped him ... add to this the fact that Bob lost his only daughter to cancer [age 22] so we share a common sorrow. He lost his only child and yours truly lost the best friend she ever had — both to cancer."

Remembering does not mean comparing, nor does it mean a constant "presence" of the former mate. It means having a healthy attitude about both the past and the present.

There should be no inhibition to talking about a former spouse (especially one who has died), incidents in your lives together, relationships with former in-laws and friends.

Doris said: "I speak of Buck freely to my husband and friends, acquaintances, etc. Discussing him with Bob comes naturally for, you see, we were neighbors and Bob used to come visit Buck almost every day. So we're really talking about 'our friend.' "

Remarriage does not mean forgetting. After all, your deceased or divorced mate was an integral part of your life whether the marriage was short or long, and it is impossible — in fact, illogical and unhealthy — to erase your own history. Your memories can enrich your life and your new relationship.

Bill said: "I think I've been very fortunate having two women in my life whom I respect. Cathy understands about Goldie and says one of the reasons she loves me is because of my loyalty. She feels I'm a good person because of it."

Cathy had been divorced 14 years before she and Bill wed. He had been widowed for two years. They have a continuing warm relationship with the family and friends who had been an integral part of Bill's and Goldie's lives. It is not unusual that talk about family birthdays, weddings, and simple day-to-day happenings would elicit Goldie's name and her participation in those activities. No one gives it a second thought and no one feels uncomfortable.

The openness about a former mate is not always easy in cases of divorce. That is especially true when there is a residue of rancor. However, in those cases, too, it is healthier to allow the references than to avoid them and thus permit anger and bitterness against the previous spouse to fester and affect the new marriage.

On the other hand, one should not feel compelled to interject the previous mate's name gratuitously; nor should one use the past for comparisons. That's a definite no-no. But you should not feel uncomfortable when the name or events arise. In fact, trying to ignore that part of your life may suppress feelings that will build and erupt at a later, inappropriate time.

That's what happened to Gloria, who was 20 when her first husband died, leaving her with an infant daughter. Her parents discouraged any talk about her pain and sadness. The man she married 18 months later let it be known he didn't want to hear about her youthful marriage. Her child grew up believing "Daddy" was her biological father.

Ten years after her second marriage, Gloria suffered an emotional collapse. It took long, painful months of therapy to reveal the cause of her anxieties, fears and blocked emotions. Once she was able to articulate her memories and dreams, and finally, complete her delayed mourning for her young husband who had died so many years before, her recovery was swift and complete.

"Being able to talk about him as someone who had lived and been a part of my life was like being relieved of a tremendous burden I'd carried all those years."

Although Molly and Jim married before she had completed the grief process following her husband's suicide, Jim understood and was supportive. A year after their marriage she told me: "We did talk about my emotional needs. Jim understands. I still have times when I need to cry; I still have times when I need to talk about Art — the death, the sickness. And I do talk about it with Jim in detail. I don't think there's much I've kept from him. There are some things — you know, you don't tell anybody everything. He's my best friend and I feel very close to him and I can say anything to him and he'll still love me. I am a very emotional person and I express my emotions. I told him all along, 'I may not be completely over this so you'll have to understand that.' After all, he was Art's friend and we have memories to share. That helps."

Jim was an especially sensitive and empathetic person. He was very patient with Molly's need to grieve. Nevertheless, that wasn't enough to hold the marriage together. It foundered after eight years.

Many people do not realize the mourning process can take as long as three years. They rush into marriage in the belief the new relationship will alleviate the sad and painful feelings. It might camouflage them for awhile, but they may emerge as inappropriate anger or frustration in the new marriage — especially if the new spouse is unaware and unsympathetic about the grief process.

A major impediment to sustained personal growth and a successful union can be a hasty remarriage before completing the mourning process.

"Too much elapsed time and too much denial make it difficult to get back in touch with those feelings which are essential for resolving and integrating a loss. A loss needs to be fully felt and expressed in order for healing and recovery to occur." (Weizman and Kamm, *About Mourning, Support and Guidance for the Bereaved.*)

Gloria was still a young woman — not yet 40 — but the pattern could be the same for her older sister, her mother or any person, man or woman, who denies the grief that is natural after the death of a loved one.

Just because your previous marriage ended in divorce, don't think you are exempt from grief. Even if you are happy to end an unpleasant, debilitating relationship, you will experience separation and change of status. That means pain and grief — unfinished psychological business to be completed before moving on to the next phase of your life.

Over the past several decades, there has been a change in attitude about the status of women, even in the over-50 age group. Judson T. and Mary G. Landis described, in *Building a Successful Marriage*, the continuing struggle between yesterday's (and, in some cases, today's) traditionalism which delineates male/female functions in marriage, and the flexibility expected by women today. The dominant-superior male ego can mean trouble unless the wife is still imbued with the old idea of wifely submission.

The attitude changes that dominate today's thinking are defined in *No Fault Marriage*, by Lasswell and Lobsenz: "Except for their biological functions, the line between male and female roles ... is blurred and elastic. The traditional sex-linked division of labor is no longer necessary, nor even practical. Few ... marry for economic reasons, for sexual availability, for social approval or out of fear of social *dis*approval ...

"We marry now for emotional fulfillment ... intellectual companionship ... shared values ... mutual psychological support, for the sense of intimacy that goes beyond superficial sex. We marry, in short, for the host of satisfactions to which we give the label 'love.' "

Lasswell and Lobsenz caution about deluding

oneself with the idea that differences will dissipate after the marriage. In fact, as they infer, what might be a minor conflict during courtship can escalate after marriage into a major breach.

If you fall into a pattern of little "lover's quarrels" and only think about the pleasures of making up instead of finding the reasons for those quarrels — the basic personality needs of each — the implications for the marriage are not very good.

"There is a very high association between premarital confidence in the relationship and the later marital happiness," the Landises say. But "every minor doubt about the future is [not] a danger signal."

One hoped-for interview for this book disappeared because the woman believed she didn't fit into the context since she had not yet married. Her problem was that her "doubts" kept interfering. Every time a date was set for the wedding, she found another excuse to postpone it.

Another tocsin sounded by the Landises is the desire to change the other person. Whether it is your desire to alter the other's behavior or his or hers to alter yours, the idea is not a good one. It weakens the foundation upon which you are planning to build the marriage. You have to accept the personality with the unpleasing traits as well as the good ones. If you don't like what you perceive, think you can change him or her, forget the whole thing. It won't work.

A good foundation begins before "I do."

A good marriage emerges when the relationship is based on a combination of love, respect, mutual interests, a pragmatic assessment of the reasons for the marriage, and working out *in advance* the areas that might cause conflict. Vital to all these is maintaining a sense of humor and a sense of balance.

Achieving an intimate relationship as gratifying as, or more gratifying (when the marriage ended in divorce) than in your previous marriage requires recognizing, working through and discarding old patterns of behavior that may have disrupted the past relationship. It is not an easy task but it will pay dividends in the new relationship.

Some marriage counselors suggest there may even be occasions when it might be best not to articulate feelings. It takes common sense to know when to withhold and when to disclose them.

Valerian J. Derlaga and Alan L. Chaikin (*Sharing Intimacies*) caution: "Sometimes withholding feelings can benefit the relationship. Nondisclosure may be the best solution, particularly if the disclosure would be perceived as threatening or punitive. Deep-seated problems need professional counseling, but open communication lines may avert that."

Humans are complex creatures with many overlapping, often ambivalent, feelings. A good marriage is not a process that homogenizes two unique individuals into one. It is an intertwining of two persons who can maintain their individuality, maturity and adaptability. Each party has a responsibility to understand and practice the spirit of compromise.

"The ability to share intimacies attests to the closeness of the couple. The partners' ability to divulge personal and even potentially embarrassing material — without fear and threat — demonstrates their respect and affection for each other."

Bernadine Kreis (*To Love Again*) supports that thesis of Derlaga and Chaikin: "... men and women need [not] be competitors ... they can unite to complement each other. They can depend upon each other emotionally, however independent they may be in tastes and interest, or even in their working lives.

"To enter into a one-to-one relationship takes courage; to make it work," Kreis continues, "takes stamina; and to keep the romance of it takes dedication."

To that end, some counselors advise the use of three watchwords — *Communication, Negotiation, Compromise* — to establish a good basis for a healthy, long-lasting relationship. Following that credo is a sensible and practical guideline.

Observance of the watchwords begins before the marriage vows are spoken. Don't expect the Good Fairy to wave her magic wand as the rings are exchanged so you can "communicate." If you haven't done it before, you're not going to find pearls of wisdom and candor suddenly dripping from your tongues after the ceremony.

Disagreements are normal, but you don't always have to win the argument. Nor do you have to swallow your feelings — anger, frustration, jealousy. Tell it straight. No name calling, no sarcasm, no underhandedness. We cause hurt when we call the other person dumb or selfish and don't say why. Such language is destructive. However, your friend (or mate) might appreciate an explanation of *why* you see the behavior in that particular situation as undesirable. In fact it would give the person an opportunity to try to correct the "misbehavior."

Real conflict, based on principles or attitudes, not on superficial ideas or beliefs, need not be destructive. Openness and verbal disagreements enlighten and clarify so both participants end up with more knowledge and strength. "Love is possible only if two persons communicate with each other ... [it] is a constant challenge." (Fromm)

So, once again, that's where the dicta of *Communication, Negotiation, Compromise* come in.

Communication

Determining whether or not you are ready for a new and lasting relationship with a particular person is not an easy task. Open communication lines are important — whether you establish them while driving in the country, walking the streets of your town or sipping coffee at your kitchen table.

Communication means *open, in-depth discussions* of convictions, religious beliefs, political ideas, family situations, personal likes and dislikes, and finances, in all their aspects — positive and negative. *It especially means talking and questioning — not trying to guess or assume what the other person has in mind.*

A classic case of lack of communication is that of Ina and Paul. She said she could not continue to live with his unpredictable moodiness, vacillation from generosity to miserliness, and never knowing whether he would laugh or scowl when he entered a room. Their separation was a sad example of what happens when there is little or no give and take between husband and wife.

Sometimes, though, our perceptions about communication can change. Ellen and Fred are a good example: in 1983, when they first responded to a questionnaire for this study, Ellen said: "We both work actively at communicating with each other; accept each other as we change and grow." At the time, they had been married five years. Each had been previously divorced for several years.

In 1990, a year after Ellen and Fred had separated and were awaiting their final divorce decree, she responded to a second questionnaire. She felt the marriage had failed because it was a "poor match emotionally from the beginning. Emotional distance widened with the years." With a tinge of bitterness, she commented: the marriage "counselor told Fred to choose between his truck and me. The truck 'won.' "

Fred, with a Ph.D. in sociology, had been a faculty member at a large midwestern university. He had become disenchanted with the academic life. After several years of marriage, he changed his career from professor to truck driver. In 1983 he said he'd married Ellen because he loved her and because he had a "desire for companionship and more regular life-style." Although his first marriage had ended in divorce, partly because of immaturity, he felt he had "learned more about myself. Also, my expectations are more realistic so I don't place so much hope for my entire happiness in the marriage [to Ellen]."

That negative attitude laid the groundwork for failure. In 1990, his reasons for the marriage failure the second time were: "job requiring great travel time; *lack of ability to communicate*; lack of common interests; *relationship started with romance rather than solid friendship*" (my italics).

This twice-divorced couple had some words of advice for those who are planning remarriage:

Ellen: "If the intended spouse's family has history of alcohol or other addictions or abuse, *stay away.*" And, "Get your own history straight before getting into a relationship. Relationships won't solve your problems."

Fred: "Be friends before lovers. Be emotionally self-sufficient and mature before marriage. Don't look at marriage as a means to solve personal problems."

They are not the only couple in my survey, and in

the numerous other studies of divorce and remarriage, where the foundation was not strong enough to weather the vicissitudes of marriage.

Molly admits: "I wasn't totally honest from the start about my feelings. Thus, no *real* communication developed. He thought he could buy me and keep me by loving me. It doesn't work unless both people are 'in love.' We had no man/woman relationship. We were only friends and in need. We didn't really love each other. I did not love him, but I loved the idea of being married."

Her divorced spouse, Jim, found two causes for their break-up. He had lost his job and Molly had not "fully resolved the death of her first husband." He suggested: "Conversation about problems is *very* important. One should listen to his heart and instincts first ... not the advice (??) of friends. Be patient during hard times (financial, emotional, etc.)."

One final example of the results of lack of communication: although Felice and her former spouse maintain a friendly business relationship — they own several businesses in partnership — their marriage of 19 years disintegrated for two main reasons: she has a great deal of intellectual curiosity and is interested in the arts. His *only* interests are sports and the businesses. In addition, she commented succinctly: "I no longer wanted to play the victim role and he could not accommodate to that."

Even though part of love is "responding to unexpressed needs," misguessing may lead to difficulties. That's why clarity is imperative. Verbal jousting to hide one's feelings and resorting to obtuse or abusive phrasing are verboten. They are a block to communication. Avoid ambiguity. You may see your point clearly but fail to make it intelligible for the other person. That is very important because some persons tend to interpret another's words to fit a personal view or prejudice. Lack of clarity may lead to speculation of meaning; misguessing the intent leads to misunderstanding, recrimination, argument. Of course, the other party has to cooperate by allowing you to explain. If the explanation is cut off too often it may lead to arguments and real trouble in the relationship.

Growing up, we learn that sometimes it is easier to suppress our own needs to please others than to invite displeasure by being honest. Some people are afraid to voice their ideas and feelings because that might evoke anger or rejection. But that fear is self-defeating and can inject a note of discord in the alliance. It is important to express your feelings — whether about how to handle your joint finances or how your partner responds to a bit of teasing.

Despite the fact that you perceive the relationship as good, you might fear rejection if you raise serious questions that really should be faced before marriage. To make the decisions, it is a good idea to explore each question openly, honestly. Good sense dictates that you come to the point without obfuscation — "We should examine our finances," "decide where we'll live," "take a good look at our likes and dislikes," "I'm happy (unhappy) you want to continue your career."

That does not mean there has to be perfect agreement on everything. Such a thought is totally unrealistic. What it calls for is examination of the nuances of possible areas of disagreement. Then try to negotiate and compromise before they become disruptive. And do it *before* the wedding bells ring.

Arthur C. Wassmer, Ph.D., gives an excellent definition of assertiveness — and that's what we're talking about: "... behaving as if you have the right to be who you are. That sounds absurdly simple until we notice how much of our behavior represents a denial of that right ... We pay lip service to attitudes and beliefs that are not really ours because we're afraid we'll be rejected if we disagree ... How cheaply we sell our birthrights of personal identity for a spurious kind of acceptance that is based on a denial of who we really are!"

For a long time, in her first marriage, Ellen sold her birthright: "My feelings were ignored ... He simply never saw my need to communicate with him, never took my changing attitudes seriously. [He] had an explosive personality. I spent a lot of time humoring him so he wouldn't yell or embarrass me."

Of course, assertiveness can be misused. There are some people who overwhelm their partners with their authoritarianism, stubbornness, or outright indifference to their spouse's feelings, so that any attempts at communication are nullified. These antics indicate that the person, no matter what age, has never grown up. Like a child, he or she feels entitled to special treatment, that his or her opinions have priority over anyone else's so there's no sense even discussing them.

This behavior often will be evident early in the relationship. The wise man or woman walks away before there is any talk of marriage.

To her sorrow, Ina ignored the early warning signals. After two years of marriage to Paul and too many stresses, the marriage disintegrated. Ina packed up and left. It was a difficult but intelligent decision that many women do not have the courage to make. Her generation of women (those born in the first third of the twentieth century and before) is not always as self-reliant and creative as she. She was able to rebuild her life as a single person on the strength of her own inner resources, her relationships with her sisters and old friends, and her cultural and social interests.

The older women who appeared on the television show *20/20* on October 19, 1990 are testimony to the fact that many who came of age and were well entrenched in marriage before the era of women's lib are unprepared to be anything but wife and mother. So, despite their discontent, they often cling to an unhappy marriage for protection instead of venturing into the broader world.

Even though Ina made the wisest choice for her own contentment, there are facets to her story which emphasize the special poignancy of the might-have-beens if communication and compromise had been effected before and during their marriage — a second for both.

It is inevitable that loss of loved ones and one's own physical infirmities multiply as the years pass, and by the time Ina had passed her 82nd birthday, the tragedies had taken their toll.

Her three sisters died; she had a cataract operation, and soon afterwards, fell and broke her hip. Instead of having a loving mate to comfort her, she spent her last months in a nursing home among strangers. She continued to be cheerful, outgoing and involved with the people around her, but underneath it all, one could sense her aloneness.

Cantankerous Paul fared better in his last years because his two daughters nurtured him during the difficult times. But the 12 years between Ina's departure and his final illness, for the most part, were empty and lonely.

Until he was 85, he continued to run his little business and his days were occupied. The evenings were a different story. He cooked and ate his solitary meal, watched a little television and slept in an empty apartment with only the haunting sound of a distant foghorn to emphasize the quiet.

The only surcease from his repeated complaints of

loneliness came from periodic visits to his two daughters, each of whom lived in distant cities. "My children mean more to me than you do," he had reminded Ina more than once. He was incapable of recognizing that each kind of love has its own place in a man's life, or to fathom the pain he inflicted with such remarks.

If Ina had used her head as well as her heart before the nuptials she probably would not have married him — or, at least, she would have known more about the man she was marrying and may have worked out strategies for averting or softening the conflicts and pain.

The sensible thing to do — instead of walking into a misalliance because you are "in love," or in an attempt to run from loneliness, financial problems, single-parenting, or whatever your motive — is to remember that "love is the active concern for the life and the growth of that which we love."

The partners must be able to share personal and even potentially embarrassing details without feeling threatened. The ability to do that will forge a stronger bond of love, mutual respect and affection.

Although it is important to understand and express your own feelings, self-awareness can lead to self-indulgence and a closing out of other people's feelings. Being able to balance your needs with the needs of the other person or persons who will be involved in the new marriage will be the gift you can give to them and to yourself.

When someone has lived without a mate for awhile — whether widowed or divorced — with children in the house or not — certain patterns of behavior take over. The person can become ego-centric, and thoughtless of someone else's feelings or needs. If that person is considering remarriage, it takes a special effort and makes good sense to heed the watchwords: *Communication, Negotiation, Compromise.*

Remember that both of you must listen. When you tune out you are doing a disservice to the union.

Negotiation and Compromise.

Webster's Third New International Dictionary (Unabridged) defines negotiate: "to communicate or confer with another so as to arrive at the settlement of some matter; meet with another so as to arrive through discussion at some kind of agreement or compromise about something; to encounter and dispose of (as a problem, challenge) with completeness and satisfaction."

The same dictionary defines compromise as "the result or embodiment of concession or adjustment; to adjust or settle (a difference) between parties; to adjust or settle by partial mutual relinquishment of principles, position or claims; settle by coming to terms (husband and wife compromised their differences.)"

So, negotiation and compromise are kissin'

cousins, tied together by kinship. Neither is possible without the other. Nor is either possible if one partner stands stubbornly entrenched in old ideas and preconceptions.

Another enemy of negotiation and compromise is false pride. It can negate any possibility of consideration of the other person's point of view. "We'll do it my way or not at all!" is a green light for a blockbuster argument.

Anger is evinced in a variety of ways: excessive criticism, withholding information even when there's no reason to; being too argumentative, or clamming up.

"The silent treatment" is an exacerbating tactic. Neither that nor the noisy battle solves anything. The "silent" caper can be the more dangerous to a relationship. At least the blockbuster argument gets the anger and hurts out in the open. But the alternative allows the bone of contention to take refuge in the subconscious where it can hibernate until another time. Nothing is solved by "forgetting about it." Hurt feelings are suppressed to reemerge at a later date and fan the flames of a new argument.

"Marriage calls for the merger of two different sets of perceptions and understanding: the working out of a real relationship calls for the dovetailing of two very different family systems."

If both parties are considerate and open to change — weighing priorities and bending or standing based on the importance of those priorities — compromises are attainable. But it all has to be talked out. Nothing is solved by ignoring the differences.

"The bond [marriage] provides a mutually shared space in the world," Maggie Scarf opines in *Unfinished Business*: "... a place of interdependent security ... Marriage is, when it operates well, a means with which the couple manages to give each other significance ... [it is the] best sort of mutual support system ... each ... bestows upon the other a sense of his or her importance and intrinsic worth."

Many psychologists and marriage counselors recommend scrutiny of the motives for remarriage, a prenuptial agreement, and (when either or both parties have children) substantive education and planning to encourage harmonious relationships. That is especially important where there are children who will be living with the newlyweds or will be "visiting" children who come for weekends, holidays and summers.

Without explicit guidelines and rules, there may not be an opportunity for good associations to develop. Quite the contrary, they may be marred by erroneous preconceptions, misunderstandings, jealousies or factionalisms and the entire family structure may suffer.

CHAPTER 4 **PROBE THE QUESTION AND PLAN FOR THE FUTURE**

Take a good look.

Psychologists and marriage counselors recommend three steps to strengthen the bonds of the marriage: close scrutiny of the motives for remarriage, a prenuptial contract, and careful planning.

It may seem unromantic, but there is no substitute for probing the question of remarriage in a slow and deliberate way. Don't just shrug and repeat Ina's words: "I love him. I like being with him." She might have averted the unhappy ending to her marriage to Paul if she had looked beyond those emotions.

And if Molly had realized she was in love with the idea of marriage — not with Jim — she first would have resolved the grief following the death of her young husband. Then she would have had a more mature perspective about her needs and the possibility of remarriage.

You are facing a decision that will affect the rest of your life, so good sense dictates that you weigh the pros and cons.

The weighing process starts with self-analysis. If

you put yourself under a microscope, you will discover things you like and some you don't. At least if you do find any unpleasant characteristics — perhaps an overabundance of self-centeredness, a short fuse on your temper, excessive pride, or other negative personality traits — determination and a bit of humility may help you attain a more satisfactory disposition.

Obviously there are different approaches to self-analysis and examination of your motives. No matter how you do it, take your time. Be thorough and honest with yourself. That's sometimes very hard to do. A person has to be willing to self-assess and change, grow up, stand back and really be self-critical even if some of the things found are hurtful.

Be a list maker.

My research uncovered three women from different areas of the country, of different ages but somewhat similar cultural and economic backgrounds, whose systems evolved into a pattern you might find helpful. Each of them used variations on the same theme. Perhaps because each had always been a list maker, the approach was natural for them. But even if you are not that organized, try it this time. You'll find it a useful tool in your search for answers.

The suggestion to be a list maker does not mean sitting down once or twice with pad and pencil and trying to enumerate your good points and bad, your motives, hopes, desires, needs, what you expect of the marriage and what you hope to bring to it. If you try that, you'll be bound to miss a few things and you might quickly also lose interest in the whole idea.

Each of the women followed the same procedure. They placed a pad and ballpoint pen (a pencil point can break just as you come up with a brilliant thought) in strategic places around the house. They put them on the desk, the bedside table, attached to the refrigerator, near their favorite chair, etc.

The working woman kept them handy in her office. All of them kept them on the dashboard or empty passenger seat of their cars for easy access when stopped for a traffic light; and the ubiquitous pad and pen were in their purses for handy use while shopping, walking, working, or lunching with friends.

All that may seem like carrying the Boy Scout credo of "Be Prepared" a bit far, but it can be the most effective weapon you have to confront the questions and ideas that will guide you toward that important verdict about the rest of your life. Often one of the most difficult things to do is recall a cogent idea that occurred an hour ago — or last night just as you were dozing off. If you jot it down when it pops into your mind (it might be slightly illegible if you do it when half asleep, but that's better than not capturing it at all), it's there in black and white for future reference.

The procedure, then, is to write down every question, every idea about yourself and what you are looking for, your good points, your shortcomings as you see them. Your ideas about stepparenting (if pertinent, of course), your feelings about the other person's children, your annoyance with certain of his or her habits or idiosyncrasies — even a true love can be upset by a minor omnipresent behavior pattern such as knuckle-cracking, slapping one on the back, pushing eyeglasses when they slip (why not have them adjusted?) — are all essential fodder for consideration.

This exercise can be continued for as long as you feel it is necessary: perhaps a week, perhaps two weeks, perhaps longer. Keep at it until you believe you have run dry. Then sort the material. You probably made repeated notes on the same theme. Consolidate them. It might take several sittings (especially if you have a full-time job) to arrive at a point where you can begin to take a good look at yourself and begin to set priorities for your desires, needs and expectations. As you delve into the many facets, your priorities will change and rearrange themselves.

Eventually you will know more about who you are, what you are seeking in the marriage and which things are most important to you. Setting priorities will give you the flexibility to compromise or even dismiss some of the less important expectations. Remember, *unrealistic* expectations can sow the seeds of disharmony.

Even if you decide against the marriage, you certainly should have gained new insights into yourself and what direction you want your life to go.

What questions do you ask?

Undoubtedly your first question will be: "What kinds of questions should I ask myself?"

There are basics for every woman faced with a marriage proposal and every man who thinks he wants to make the proposal.

Also, there are some that are unique to middle-aged and older persons.

This chapter and those that follow are not meant to be the font of all wisdom. Nor are they all-encompassing. They are posed to point you in the proper direction with the idea that, once stimulated, the impetus will help you develop your own expertise. So look upon these questions as only a beginning; the follow-through is up to you.

Remember, all couples go through a period of learning and adjusting. Many older people are taking a page from the lifestyle of their children. They are opting for living together for awhile — maybe only a couple of months, maybe even as long as several years. This could be a period of discovery — an opportunity to iron out some of the wrinkles in their relationship. But there's no guarantee. Research has shown that the living-together time may run smoothly, but then hidden problems develop after the wedding ceremony. Or the arrangement may be so satisfactory the couple decides to forego marriage altogether.

There can be pitfalls in an LTA (living together arrangement) that might not occur to the parties involved until problems (emotional or even legal) arise. Then it could be too late. Financial aspects of LTAs are reviewed in *Chapter 8, Financial Security, Wills and Pre- or Postnuptial Agreements.*

For those who opt for an LTA as a temporary arrangement to be followed by marriage, there are words of caution, too. Occasionally, the marriage ceremony may cause an unexpected change of attitude by the spouses to the detriment of the relationship.

Mel Krantz in *Learning to Love Again* offers a discerning examination of this special problem. If you are presently in an LTA and contemplating marriage, that chapter of his book offers useful information. Even if the LTA runs smoothly, questions may develop after the wedding ceremony and reading those few pages in the Krantz book will alert and prepare you for dealing with them.

Whether you choose the "modern" alternative or step right up to marriage, it's a matter of determination, luck, timing and patience before one learns how a relationship is going to work out.

You will find that the dynamics of remarriage really differ very little from the struggles in your first marriage. But if you are mature enough and willing to confront the many facets of marriage beforehand, you will smooth the way to compatible companionship and contentment.

After a divorce, it takes courage to make a second marriage work. That's why congenial remarrieds are a special breed. You, too, can become a part of that special breed. All it takes is some good sense, patience and flexibility.

First, a few questions for all prospective brides and bridegrooms:

- Have you completed the emotional separation from your previous spouse, whether widowed or divorced?

- If you were divorced, why didn't the other marriage work? Was the separation your fault, his, or were both of you at fault? Was it inexperience, lack of maturity?

The participants in this study claimed, almost without exception, that they were either too young and inexperienced, or even if older in years, too immature at the time of their first marriage. Lack of communication, also, was given as a dominant reason for the break-up.

Even some of those whose first marriages were ended by death after 10,15, 20 years confessed to similar problems. But they stayed married, made the best of it, even considered themselves "happily" married because they worked out patterns to deal with the incompatibilities.

Marie's explanation was different from most of the

others: "... [in the previous marriage] we were striving to reach goals. In this marriage we are enjoying them."

Becky pointed out: "We were the wrong two people together. He didn't want to be Jewish-connected. He had affairs, but he was not in balance in any relationship."

But Ronnie, like a majority of the respondents, said: "Immaturity, inability to communicate, disagreement on money management, incompatibility of values." She added another probability: "... a gap in education — he was an M.D., I was not a college graduate at that time."

Carol said: "Disagreement over my role in the marriage. He wanted a traditional wife; I felt trapped in such a role."

Tom reported that in both of his previous marriages there were conflicts over money, children, extra-marital affairs — often brought on because of immaturity of both parties.

Bob's reasons were lack of communication, immaturity, conflict of interests.

- What do you expect to get from this marriage? Love, companionship, someone to take over the burden of finances because you are hopelessly mired in numbers? Or are you looking for prestige, social status, lots of travel or pretty clothes, a parent for your children?

Molly's needs seemed to encompass most of those

reasons. She said about her remarriage only a few months after her first husband committed suicide: "I was lonely. I loved the state of marriage and wanted it again. I wanted a father for my children and a husband and a lover and a provider." She wanted utopia but she had not completed her mourning and was not ready for remarriage. It was the desire to recapture the happy state of togetherness that, despite a loving and solicitous second husband (see *Chapter 3*), made their "ideal" marriage a relatively short one. Three years after her divorce from Jim, she continues to seek a happy marriage. "I am okay," she told the interviewer, "but I do not like being single at all. I read a lot of books on what one 'should' do to have a happy and healthy relationship/marriage, but I just have not found the right partner!"

On the other hand, Becky's second marriage has prospered for more than 25 years. She said: "We have grown and developed in parallel harmonious fashion based on respect and encouragement." They both worked at interesting careers while raising his and her children from previous marriages and one of their own. Now they are enjoying grandparenthood and continuing their careers.

John was typical of those in their mid-60s and older. His desire was companionship and an intimate relationship. He wanted someone to travel with and enjoy the good life.

- What do you expect to give? Warmth, companionship, compassion, parenting for his/her children, financial cooperation, a helping hand in the other's business or career, your ability to solve problems — financial, emotional?

- Do you love the person — really love him or her? Love is a sharing of hopes, dreams, feelings, accepting each other and working out problems.

Ronnie said: "[with my second husband] I think it must have revolved around the good sex we had. This I never had before — as I look back. I really believed I loved the man — though now I wonder how could I? He was very attentive, interesting but controlling. He 'knew what was good for me'! ... I must have been blinded by the need to love and be loved."

- Do you long for a permanent emotional connection? If so, is this it or are you fooling yourself? Samuel Johnson pointed out: "Marriage has many pains, but celibacy has no pleasures." And, for the moment, your sexual need might be distorting your perception.

- Is it because you enjoy the ego-massage of having someone attentive and loving? Many of the respondents denied that. On the contrary, they claimed, the relationship went deeper than that. The second marriage, they contended, was more balanced, without the needs of one dominating and leading to the neglect of the other person's needs.

Bob called his first wife a "Jewish Princess," the present one "a doll!"

Doris, his present wife, said: "Buck [deceased first husband] was self-oriented, Bob is other-oriented. Although the two men are as different as day and night, in both instances they were/are my entire world."

Alice said: "This marriage is totally different. The responsibilities are grown-up, we both have matured and things that we thought were important in our younger days are not any more."

Marie said: "He's very confident — makes me feel I'm the most important thing in his life. My first husband was just the opposite."

But Ronnie said: "He just came into my life and took over!"

- Are you certain you won't mind giving up some of your independence? This is an especially difficult adjustment for independent career women and those who have lived alone for a long time. They have set schedules — or lack of them — and life patterns that may demand a lot of self-discipline for adapting to a new mode of life. It may mean seeing less of special friends and having to spend time with the other's friends who don't exactly please you.

Ronnie reported: "I introduced him to several of

my friends. He usually had some destructive criticism. We were friends with his favorite couple for years until he [my husband] broke it off. We moved from the L.A. area and I gave up seeing my friends. The distance didn't help."

Carol and Tom, however, typify many of the men and women in the survey. She told me: "Almost without exception, we've accepted each other's friends, although we're not afraid to say what we dislike about them."

Cathy and Bill agree. She said: "There are very few, if any, friends either of us have that we cannot like or tolerate." He said: "We didn't give up friends but changes do occur because of natural philosophical differences with certain acquaintances."

Alice's experience was quite the opposite: "My husband gave up a family of friends when he found they disapproved of me." Fred showed great consideration for her feelings: "I made the choice to drop my old friends since I felt it was important for her to be comfortable and make friends easily."

Women are not the only ones faced with dilemmas. Men, too, may react negatively or expect the new spouse to make all the adjustments, leaving him with his idiosyncrasies and desires and ignoring hers.

"I don't know why I never stressed this," Ronnie admitted, "but I had so little time to myself — he was always home — summer, winter! After a few years I really began to resent it ... as he did not work outside the home, the demands on me were often overwhelming — I became very resentful, even though he did keep busy and did a tremendous amount of work on the property ... he did help with cleaning and laundry — he also kept the cars in good running condition ... " Despite his helpfulness around the house and property, he was always there — never giving Ronnie any time to herself, smothering her with his presence and cutting her off from old friends.

- Are you willing to accept the fact that he is a stickler for tidiness while you tend to leave panties and hose on the bathroom floor? What if he's the untidy one and you're a fanatical picker-upper?

- Can you relax while she's driving the car? Is it a subject you can talk about and try to find a compromise? It would be awful to spend the rest of your years riding with clenched fists because she drives too aggressively for your peace of mind.

- Or is he derisive of your caution behind the wheel? And how do you respond to that?

- Do you like opera while he prefers country music, which drives you up the wall? That should be an easy one for compromise: you can attend the opera alone or with a friend and he can make his own plans for hearing his kind of music. If either of you wants to listen to records or the radio, plan it so the other person is out of the house or occupied with a different project at the time.

- Are you willing to negotiate and compromise on other points of dissension in exchange for the companionship and someone to share the good and bad times?

Who are you and what are you looking for?

Now it is time for an assessment of your own personality, habits and hang-ups. If you don't do this work before your final decision, you may find unexpected things happening after the honeymoon.

Self-disclosure is important to establish and maintain a good relationship. That means taking a very close look at yourself, your behavior, your thought processes, your credos, your principles, and how you respond to negative and good events in your life and in your interpersonal relationships.

The preceding examination is the beginning. There are other areas to be scrutinized.

Some persons can't cope with hearing negative things about themselves. Is this one of your shortcomings? Are you willing to face this possibility in your new marriage and learn to deal with it gracefully?

Or are you one who tends toward sarcasm, derision and hurtful remarks? Some persons think they're being funny when they use these tactics to express disagreement or discontent. It's not funny to the person who is the target. If something displeases you, it is important to discuss it rather than suppress feelings, but there are better ways to discuss it than with truculence.

Consider the following words and phrases. What comes to mind about yourself when you consider these *positives and negatives*?

POSITIVES
commitment and cooperation
empathy
ability to work through problems in a
constructive way
objectivity
emotional maturity
partnership to enrich life
respect, encouragement
understanding motivations
taking responsibility for mistakes
thinking independently
voicing your point of view
sense of proportion about present desires
and future goals
sacrifice for others

NEGATIVES
feelings of martyrdom when you give up your
time, energy, money to help someone

disappointment and disillusion about how the
partnership could go (or is going) — can lead
to deterioration of the relationship

occasional serious differences may precipitate a crisis — do you "clam up," or get nasty?

sudden unexpected, or a build-up, of emotional tension because of evasion of differences

lack of understanding of what marriage means, including the importance of communication, negotiation and compromise

Honest self-analysis will uncover your strengths and weaknesses in these areas and may help you make readjustments in your thinking. When dissension or arguments arise in the future, you will be prepared. Then you can choose the time and the words to discuss them. Being able to balance your needs with the needs of the other person (or persons) involved in the marriage will be a boon to all of you.

There are several other subjects for examination:

1. Is your new choice like your previous spouse? How are they different? Too often individuals do not realize they are marrying the mirror images of their first spouses. Sometimes that works out okay. But too often it is disastrous. So take a good look!

2. If your previous marriage ended in divorce, what were the reasons for the failure? Your fault, his, both of you?

3. Before or during the previous marriage did

you communicate, discuss problems? Are you talking now with your new friend about mutual interests, ideas about sex, religion, finances, politics, interest in arts, sports, literature, sharing responsibilities, the need for individual privacy, job conflicts, children, etc.?

Don't confront any of these matters casually. *This is your future you're playing with*, and it will be no laughing matter if you come up with a hasty, wrong answer. The questions need clear and pragmatic answers and the ability to be adaptive when contrary opinions surface.

The essence of the marriage contract is accepting your partner "for better or for worse." It is true that we can't always be held responsible for what we feel, but a mature person must accept responsibility for his or her behavior. So it behooves you, if you are contemplating remarriage, to make certain you are ready to accept that responsibility.

Loneliness can be a terrible thing, but being willing to forego some of your freedom can also be difficult.

Unless you are convinced you are able to accept some significant changes in your lifestyle, you'd best reconsider your choice between remarriage and continued singleness, including the loneliness that goes with it.

The takers, the givers and the vultures

There seem to be four kinds of people, whether

married or unmarried: there are "takers" and "givers," and there are those who are able to balance their relationships with others so that neither characteristic is dominant.

Then, too, there are the "super-takers," the "vultures." We'll discuss them later.

Some people, without even realizing it, seek out companions who will gratify their need to dominate. They subtly — or not so subtly — bend their partners to their own will. Very often, the partner isn't aware that he or she is being used. Some who become aware may decide to live with it, or they bide their time before remedying the situation because they are fearful of arousing the anger of the spouse by broaching the subject. Others, when they've had it up to here, finally opt for divorce.

Occasional thoughtlessness or rudeness occurs in any relationship. But when such behavior occurs frequently, it indicates the person believes he or she is entitled to obeisance. It is like a small child who is wily enough to play on a parent's guilt feelings to get his way. Except this is the adult world and the taker has not grown up. This type of person suffers very little guilt himself when he uses others.

Ronnie reported: "I was older, more experienced, better educated, but I allowed him to control my life for at least 15 years. I took care of him most of our married life and I had thought he was the 'strong' one ... He lost his job and did not actively seek another. Physical and mental problems interfered. I ended up supporting us on my teacher's salary and he was directing my life. I had a hard time being me and doing what I thought I wanted." Then she came up with the contradiction — or excuse — so often added to the listing of the ways the taker controlled the life of the giver. She said: "However, I was happy." It took a long time — 20 years, in fact — before she admitted to herself that she was not happy and finally ventured to take control of her life.

It wouldn't have mattered how short or long a time Paul had been alone — one year or ten. He was a stubborn, self-centered man who had been alone for three years. His first wife had, over their 40-year marriage, alternately indulged and ignored his moods that swung like a pendulum from good to impossible.

When his daughter tried to prepare Ina for what she would face, her answer was, "I love him. In my 20 years of widowhood I haven't responded to a man the way I do to your father."

She thought her sunny disposition and compromising nature would help her cope with his cantankerousness.

This was a more naive time, when people were less aware that there might be ways to analyze problems and work out a plan for dealing with them before they became major sources of irritation.

Even if she had realized that he was a taker — of

her affection, her kindness — she might have made the same decision. But she had not seen (or she turned a blind eye to) the negative side of his personality during their courtship.

Both Paul and Ina were in their late 60s and neither was aware of the benefits that might have accrued to their marriage if they had talked about his erratic moods and his jealousy of her attachment to her sisters (a subject he never mentioned before the wedding). If Ina had been more malleable, perhaps the marriage would have survived. But, because she was unwilling to be used, the marriage was doomed before they said, "I do."

Paul was one species of taker. There are others.

There are those who appear to be givers. They are the ones who lavish their partners with gifts or an overwhelming show of affection. But that only masks their belief in their entitlement to unlimited giving by their partners — of affection, of services, or deference to their every desire or need — regardless of their mates' needs and desires.

Another kind of taker is the "sweet little woman" or the "model husband" who subtly manipulates the mate by whatever means at hand in order to gain the desired end, meanwhile remaining totally insensitive to the other's feeling or reactions. The 1991 movie, *Mr. and Mrs. Bridge,* seemed to be about a "loving couple." Actually, the wife was loving and submissive; the husband insensitive to her emotional needs.

Sometimes, consciously or unconsciously, the taker has a special antenna that can pick out someone with the need to be a giver.

Givers are usually not difficult to spot. They, too, come in different varieties.

There are those who genuinely love to be obliging.

Others wallow in their self-sacrifice. There's the wife and mother who will do anything to avoid imposing on husband or child. Everything is possible no matter how tired she may be. She gives so much she becomes dominant in the household. But sometimes that backfires. A couple of the women interviewed on the aforementioned *20/20* TV program about divorce in later life admitted they'd spent so much time being homemakers and mothers they'd lost their husbands. The result was that they gave more than they'd bargained for and more than should be expected in a good marriage.

The genuine givers are those who provide love, service, nurturance and beneficence without giving up personal pride and individuality.

So, getting back to the business of your self-analysis, this is another compelling facet of your character to examine.

Are you a giver or a taker? Is your lover a giver or a taker? These are questions best confronted on your own and, later, with the other person. Then you will be able to understand each other's positions before you fall into roles that could cause unhappiness.

Ina's and Paul's story accentuates the importance of mutual understanding and the ability to compromise to make a marriage work. *But both partners must participate.* There are differences and disagreements in every relationship, but competence and skill for working out conflicting stances keeps a marriage viable and happy.

Erich Fromm describes some so-called "happy" marriages as a smoothly functioning team — not too different from a smoothly functioning office staff. He asserts that a "well-oiled relationship between two persons who remain strangers ... may be a refuge from loneliness." Such an alliance may be mistaken for love and intimacy and it may work for some people. But that smooth-working partnership may also become a bitter, ascerbic marriage and that can be worse than loneliness.

Beware the vultures.

When I was a little girl (a long time ago), New York newspapers titillated the usually staid, often prudish, reading public in my small home town with tales of real life "gold-diggers" and their "sugar-daddies."

They were the beautiful young women who married rich old men for the luxuries they would provide. And when the men refused to marry them, the women sued for "breach of promise." Those women were the ultimate vultures — but, then, the prey was willing, as long as they believed they were profiting from the relationships. So the men, too, were vultures.

Such stories rarely make the pages of newspapers today. (Although the big social news in the fall of 1990 was that Ivana Trump was suing for divorce after 17 years of marriage to real estate entrepreneur Donald Trump, to, among other reasons, collect the $25 million stipulated in their marriage contract.)

Nevertheless, it behooves middle-aged and older men and women to remember that there are vultures out there — birds that stalk vulnerable prey. One need not be wealthy to become quarry for someone looking for a soft touch.

Lonely men and women who have comfortable incomes are vulnerable to the charms of clever takers. These vultures frequent the resorts and cruise ships that are favorite vacation choices of older persons. They exert their special talents toward a marriage that will allow them to enjoy life without contributing their fair share.

There are those who would pooh-pooh the idea that such chicanery exists in this enlightened age. But it does. You can see it in the unhappy faces of some remarrieds who have been too trusting. And some cases in the divorce courts attest to it.

Then there are women like Ginny, who are trying to work out the problem. She knows John did not marry her for her money, even though she admits "I have over twice [as much as he] and he does not want to split expenses 50-50. We are working this out. I think — I hope." They did sign a prenuptial agreement and "he is gentle and enjoys doing things for me. He caters to my every need." Except she feels he is not living up to the proviso in the agreement that they should share the household costs equally. Since he enjoys cooking, they agreed he would take care of the cost of feeding them. But when they went out to dinner he kept a careful account of her costs and insisted upon collecting for them. That wasn't how she saw the arrangement. The cost of food was his part of the bargain, and she finally insisted that his obligation didn't end when they entered a restaurant.

John's perspective on the subject was slightly different: "We are both financially secure," he told me. "Expenses are shared." Apparently there's a breakdown in their communications — but she's working on it.

Although avoiding a one-sided financial set-up is not the only reason for a prenuptial agreement, it certainly is one of the considerations for that step which will be discussed in more detail in a later chapter.

Men: take a good look too!

It is crucial that men, as well as women, take a good hard look at themselves and their plans. They are just as vulnerable to wrong decisions to remarry as are women. A man may misjudge emotional response or sexual needs as a good reason.

He could be terribly wrong.

He could be terribly wrong, too, if he is denying himself the opportunity to find another mate.

A decision to avoid "getting involved" may be because he believes he has nothing to offer — whether sexually, intellectually or socially. These feelings may be based on unresolved problems in his previous marriage or because health problems require medications that can cause impotence.

It is unfortunate if a man's fear of sexual inadequacy turns him away from developing a new relationship.

Gail Sheehy, in *Pathfinders*, explored the subject of sex. She pointed out: "People who remarry in middle age or later generally say that they are looking for companionship more than anything else. What they usually get as a bonus is a splendid sexual resurgence."

When Paul told his adult daughter about his forthcoming marriage, he admitted: "I never thought I could feel this way again. I really believed sex was over for me, but it isn't. I feel a resurgence of all those feelings I almost forgot about."

Sheehy continued her discourse on the subject: "Sexual *tempo* (italics hers) does begin to change very gradually as they get older. For people who remain healthy in body and outlook, and who maintain regular sexual relations once or twice a week, there is no decline in the quality of lovemaking." Even if lovemaking becomes less frequent — perhaps two or three times a month — that is not an indication of lessening ardor. It is simply a sign that the accumulating years do make a difference.

What the man should avoid is overreacting to the normal gradual changes taking place. That can bring on a belief that he is impotent when, in reality, he is not.

Nevertheless, good sense indicates he should consult his doctor. The condition might be psychological. But it might not. It could be medically correctable with hormone treatment. Or it might be traceable to medications or disease such as diabetes or heart disease.

Sexual inadequacy probably is the least important of his concerns. Although sex is important, and sexual activity can continue into the eighth decade for some persons, it is not an imperative for a loving and companionable relationship. If a man allows himself to become involved with a warm and caring woman, she will not reject him because of diminished sexual ability.

As for a man feeling intellectually or socially inadequate, that, too, can be a hang-up without foundation. There are men with great mental acuity who think they get failing marks when it comes to social badinage or intellectual discourse. It takes a good woman to help him overcome such feelings, but no one can help if he doesn't give himself the opportunity to socialize with women, and perhaps find the one who will be happy to help with his problems.

Those are some of the reasons a man might *avoid* remarriage. There are also possible reasons for a misconceived decision *to* remarry. Among them are the possibility he is denying or suppressing grief for a recently deceased wife or anger over a divorce; he may dislike the need to take care of the "womanly" tasks that had always been done for him; or there could be any of a dozen other reasons.

The most insidious justification for remarriage is when the attentions of women flatter his ego. Oh, how some men love to be sought after and pampered. (I'm not a female chauvinist; I admit there are lots of women like that, too.) And not all are sensible enough to separate the fun from reality.

They could take a lesson from Bill: "I felt kind of foolish," he said about dating after his wife died. "You feel that you're competing with the kids. You look at yourself and think it's all kid stuff. I didn't have anything to prove. I didn't have to be 'macho.' I'm certainly not the macho looking person," this short, balding, sweet, gentle and self-effacing man remarked with a broad grin," and my desire to conquer women or go out was an irrelevant thing. I guess I felt complimented because women would call me. That is *great* for the ego. It's also embarrassing, as far as I'm concerned.

"I got a different perspective of women," he continued with a slight note of surprise. "Women who were very nice, cultured, well educated, they wanted to go on vacations — meet away from their own environment. I didn't have to call for dates. They called me. But I wasn't sure what I was looking for. But one thing I wasn't looking for was sex.

"Maybe I was too bashful," he admitted shyly. He confessed that even a year after he finally did marry, some women continued to make overtures "in case things don't work out," they told him.

Bill had the intelligence not to mistake the awakening of sexual response and enjoyment of female company as the basis for remarriage. But another man might allow his ego to overcome his good sense. A man may be flattered by the attention lavished on him because he is one of a very special group, that scarce social commodity: the extra man. All those invitations, hostesses clamoring for his presence, women eager to accept his invitations to dinner, theater, ball games, his *bed* may cause a man to lose perspective.

The oft-told tales volunteered to me by male acquaintances and relatives, plus those interviewed, make it unmistakably clear that men pretty much can take their pick from among the eager available women. It is, however, the overabundance that might make them unwary prey for the most calculating female — one of the vultures.

But if the woman who catches him is smart, she'll examine her own motives before entering into the uncertainties of marriage without knowing as much as possible about herself and her man.

Marriage is a joint affair: confront important issues together.

The idea of so much introspection and, eventually, involving the man or woman you love in what may seem like the "third degree," might make one think the whole thing is cold-blooded. Others might consider it an invasion of privacy.

Still others might scoff that anyone going to such lengths is a little off his or her rocker. The idea is not as invasive or ridiculous as the uninitiated might believe. Don't equate this procedure with distrust even if you are told that if you really love your intended you would just trust him or her to do the right thing.

None of that is true. If the love is strong, or the desire for a companionable and compatible relationship is sincere, both persons should be willing participants in an amiable examination of the many facets of marriage before the fact. The procedure could disclose possible areas of dispute and ways to avoid them before they happen, or at least soften their impact.

Janice was particularly vehement on the subject. She urged me to please have a place in the book for "... a warning of not rushing into a new marriage. When a person had a good marriage and then suddenly is alone, it takes a great deal of healing. I am still having a hard time, especially when the problems of life become heavy. Dick was there. John is not, the leader is me and sometimes I need to lean too." In fact, despite some rough times, at the time of our interview, she was hopeful that their problems could be solved. "I care more for John now than I did when I married him. He rushed me too much and too fast. I love him very different[ly] than I loved Dick.

"I prayed for patience and God sent me John. I'm now *learning* patience."

However, during a follow-up interview several months later, she admitted she couldn't continue. The marriage was annulled but they continue to be on good terms. He visits her frequently, they've vacationed together and he was kind and helpful when she was ill. But when he's in her home he pays his way. "He really is a child in many ways and his intellectual interests fall far short of mine. I just couldn't put up with it any longer even though I am very fond of him. The new arrangement — with him as a guest in my home — my health is better."

Janice is not alone in regretting that she rushed headlong into a new marriage. My research disclosed others, including especially the unhappy marriage of Ina and Paul and the problems that led to the dissolution of the unions of Ellen and Fred and Molly and Jim.

Ronnie suggests it might not be such a bad idea to listen to the family or friends — or grown children. As she realized years later: "There may be some *good* reason for their feelings." She also asserts: "Don't give up your individuality. Stay true to yourself."

Felice urges: "I always say beware of experts. Each case is different. But I guess the most important thing is communication and honesty. That and accepting who you are and who he or she is."

Molly, who, although she continues to yearn for marriage, has grown wiser: "... I depend a lot on 'dates' for social life and I do not like that need. However, I also do not like being alone." But, she recommends: "Make sure you really love and are committed to the institution of marriage; don't marry for need or when you are not feeling good about yourself and your life; communicate everything — all the good and all the bad!"

So now is the time to bring your fiancé or fiancée into the process. And now is the time when the three watchwords — *Communication, Negotiation, Compromise* — will be of the utmost importance.

Despite what you perceive to be a good relationship, undoubtedly there are sensitive areas. If, like Ronnie ("Sometimes I was silent, afraid if I said how I felt, he'd take it all wrong.") you fear anger or rejection if you raise serious questions before the marriage, try to imagine how much more difficult it will be afterwards.

To dispel the possibilities of misapprehensions and misunderstandings, each question should be explored honestly, openly. Don't be afraid to come to the point: "We'll examine our finances together." "I'll go to church with you if you'll respect my feelings about religion." "We should be aware of each other's health problems." "I'll expect you to do your fair share of the household chores." "Since we both work, we'll have to plan our schedules and avoid conflicts when those schedules occasionally have to be scrapped."

There is a myriad of questions and it is best to confront differences, concerns, misconceptions and preconceived ideas before the marriage. *After the marriage they may disrupt all of the relationships within the reconstituted family.*

Involve your future mate in the process.

So, after your own self-examination, it is time to enlist the other person's help to get his or her assessments, evaluations, fears and feelings about the future.

Follow the pattern of your own exercise, but this time do it together. Talk about the routine you followed, the questions you asked, the answers you found and seek your intended spouse's cooperation in a similar joint effort. It might take some diplomacy to reassure the person and help him or her understand your motives.

If you're hesitant about broaching the subject, you might gain understanding and cooperation by giving your prospective mate this book to read. Then you might find it helpful to read parts of it together. This ought to help him or her realize why you feel so strongly about examining these matters before your wedding.

Once that hurdle is passed, don't obfuscate. Be stalwart, open-minded and open-hearted and always try to maintain your sense of humor. Nevertheless, and despite the first watchword for a good marriage — *Communication* — don't forget that no matter how candid you may try to be, there *are*, occasionally, some things that are private, that you are reluctant to discuss with your mate in order to avoid adverse or hurt feelings, or to protect the other person from fear of some kind.

Of course *you* have to make a decision about what is worthwhile discussing and what is best forgotten.

Nevertheless, it is important to define what each of you needs as an individual. Are you an introvert or extrovert? Do you need a constant display of affection? Do you need constant companionship or prefer some time alone? Are you a social butterfly and your intended spouse tends toward misanthropy? Do you prefer quiet dinners at home or dining out?

These are only a few possible emotional and physical needs. As you talk and interact, many others will come up.

It pays, too, to talk about the ordinary things each one likes and dislikes — the little idiosyncrasies like no ketchup bottles on the table, every picture on the wall must be straight, a dislike of opera or a passion for Bach. Discussion about little things may reveal stubbornness or, on the contrary, a willingness to compromise.

It is helpful to know each other's values and principles and how strongly the person will defend them. Discovering conflicts and dealing with them beforehand can avert unhappiness or clashes later on.

Consider what good things you want to preserve from your life as a single person. What do you need/want from the marriage? What can you give to the marriage?

Take the issues one at a time and negotiate your differences — or decide they're unimportant.

"Yes, we discussed [our separate needs and expectations] a great deal," Doris explained, "for he was married to a frigid woman and was/is thrown for a loop by my openness and warmth, and it's wonderful to see him slowly 'open up' to this side of life. We are both other-oriented types who try to please one another, so this works out simply great.

"Among his many hobbies," she continued, "he is an amateur photographer, so we share an art interest. Matter of fact, we were out early this morning taking pictures of an old barn. I'll use it in a painting or six, and he'll do likewise in his photographs. A nice blending of talent here. We both bowl and play golf. Haven't done this together as yet. He's a much better cook than I am, that's for sure. On a personality level, I'm neat and tidy and he's not, so I just follow behind and pick up after him. My dear first husband was like this so I'm well trained in *this* art. He shines when it comes to major decisions and I'm a former cost accountant, so detail comes easily for me."

To reach that kind of rapport may call for a few difficult decisions that may cause inner conflict. "It is," as Saul Friedlander wrote in *When Memory Comes*, "absolutely imperative to distinguish between the ephemeral and the essential: the ephemeral leaves its painful marks, the essential still remains. Until the day when the ephemeral has eaten away so much of the essential that the nucleus itself is destroyed."

These are personal agonies that have to be worked through, integrated, and finally put side, so there remain few hidden or unexpected causes for friction in your marriage.

CHAPTER 5 HEALTH: AN IMPORTANT CONSIDERATION

One of the issues to be confronted together is the state of your health. When one is young, the idea that health might play an important role in marriage rarely gets much thought.

But when the middle or later years creep up, the little aches and pains emerge, and you begin to learn the names of mysterious drugs, the reality has to intrude.

That does not mean the idea of marriage has to be abandoned because either or both of you has some physical ailment — arthritis, allergies, diabetes, a heart condition, etc. It is ridiculous to think that one can attain the age of 50 or 60 without sooner or later experiencing some diminution from the healthy specimen you were at age 35 or 40.

It's called the aging process, and eventually it happens to all of us. When it occurs depends upon genes, environment, health routines and a variety of other factors.

In today's world, most people are well aware of new ideas and advances in health care. In newspapers, magazines, books and on radio and television there is a proliferation of articles and programs to view or hear that inform about developments in research, new medications, current recommendations for keeping fit, etc., etc.

Substantial increases in life expectancy from the time of our grandparents and parents give a new perspective on chronic illnesses and their treatments that allow for physical activity way beyond what was once considered old age.

Men and women in their 70s, 80s, and some even into their 90s are mentally alert and often still playing tennis and golf, swimming, walking, traveling.

Positive attitudes about diet, exercise, life style, are a part of today's approach to living.

All of these factors are important when couples in their middle or late years are making plans to wed. Chronic illness, even a serious one, should not be a deterrent to active years beyond semi- or full retirement. It might mean reassessing behavior and maybe slowing down a bit but it certainly doesn't mean turning away from life. The later years can be years of exploration, education and enthusiasm, especially if they are shared with a compatible companion.

One does, however, have to be realistic about the state of health whether or not you are considering marriage. The calendar continues to discard the pages of our lives and it's nice to know they're not being discarded indiscriminately.

Some people age gracefully, face up to any health problems (minor or major in nature) and continue to live with pleasure and panache. No matter what their ailments, they enrich their own lives and the lives of anyone they touch.

Doris was aware that Bob had suffered a serious heart attack a couple of years before their marriage, but believed it would not hinder their union. She was rewarded with 11 years of happiness before his death.

Sometimes, though, someone uses illness, chronic, minor or serious to become the focus of attention. That may disrupt the household and the relationship. So it is sensible to be aware of a person's attitude about illness and disability.

That doesn't mean one should run the other way when someone seems to worry too much about minor ailments. Even hypochondria — abnormal concern over one's health — may be ignored unless it is too intrusive on normal activities. It may be only a source of gentle amusement in the relationship if it is understood and everyone retains a sense of humor.

There are times, however, even when one is aware of an ailment, the possibility of problems is waved aside by love.

When Emma and Alan married, she was aware that he was a manic-depressive. She loved him and was confident the illness would not affect their marriage. He was taking lithium, a prescription drug that controls the mood swings symptomatic of the sickness. There was no problem until he was forced into retirement by his employer. Overwhelmed by the status change, he refused professional help, and against all reason, discontinued his medication. His manic and depressive periods became unpredictable. What began with so much optimism and joy deteriorated to the point where divorce was the only solution.

Sadly, there was no way for Emma to know how the marriage would fare. Alan might have continued his treatment and the marriage would have lived up to her expectations.

One should not construe from her experience that marriage must be avoided if there are health problems. That is a silly conclusion. There are many good remarriages where one or both of the parties have ailments. A lot of the trouble develops because one or the other has been less than honest about health.

For instance, maybe one of the couple loves to cook. If the spouse failed to inform about a dietary restriction, there could be some unhappy moments until the cook learns to avoid the harmful dishes. Perhaps that wouldn't cause a major upheaval, but it could cause some unhappy moments. However, if high blood pressure, diabetes, heart disease or other disability is not discussed, a serious onslaught may impose stress beyond normal expectations.

Knowledge about an existing condition, on the other hand, can encourage a closer, more caring relationship.

Whether or not either of you has a health problem, the best approach to peace of mind is to proceed with your annual physical examinations — a ritual that has become routine for most people over 40. Then you can discuss the results with your doctors and talk over any questions that may arise.

If either of you has some kind of problem that is not life-threatening and can be controlled by diet, exercise, medication, your life style might be slightly changed, but you certainly don't have to eliminate all pleasurable activities.

A possible exception may be an illness that is the forerunner of total disability. In that case, confront the realities. The impact on the relationship would depend on the individuals.

One couple (each widowed) decided to marry despite the fact that she had to undergo dialysis three times a week. He was tender, caring; she had great emotional strength and a sense of humor that helped both of them through difficult times. In the few months they had together, they were able to travel (with pre-arranged hospital care along the way), entertain, enjoy each other's company.

No one can decide for you. But you cannot make a determination unless you know about your own health and your prospective spouse's. And, in most cases, the scenario will not be as delicately painful nor foreordained as the case cited. Diabetes, heart disease, arthritis and other manageable illnesses should not interfere with a relationship based on mutual interests and compatibility.

Know and understand your health problems, medications and regimens.

To begin, each of you must know and understand your own physical or emotional weaknesses and how you control them.

It is of utmost importance that you know about each of the medications you are taking, their interactions and side effects. Your pharmacist may be more helpful than your doctor in these areas. The pharmacist keeps a computerized record of all your medications and is knowledgeable about them. That is why it is wise to have all prescriptions filled at the same place, especially if you consult with more than one specialist.

Even though older people may react differently than the young to certain drugs, there presently is no requirement for the manufacturers of such products to inform the consumer. Some druggists enclose with your prescription printed material that is supposed to inform consumers but the information, when available, is not always helpful.

In March 1990, the Food and Drug Administration (FDA), the government agency that approves the sale of drugs, issued a guideline encouraging drug companies to evaluate the effects of drugs on people over 65. This information is to be included with the prescription. If there is no research data available, that fact would have to be stated.

Dorothy L. Smith, president of the Consumer Health Information Corporation in McLean, Virginia, was quoted in the *New York Times* (12/1/90) in connection with the suggestion that most of the material enclosed with prescriptions cannot be understood by the lay consumer, even if the small print could be read. "My concern is that there is more than just handing out a list of tips to patients," she said. "I think that older persons need practical and concise instructions in language they can understand."

Daniel Thursz, president of the National Council on the Aging, quoted in the same article, felt the FDA proposal did not go far enough. "If the information is in 4-point type on a leaflet nobody can read packed into the container, that's not going to be very effective." He recommended that the FDA add a requirement to make labels easier to read.

"Most older people have vision problems and can get confused about their various prescription drugs," he said.

The article, written by Leonard Sloane, pointed out that only 12% of the U.S. population is over 65, "but they consume more than 30 percent of prescription drugs and 40 percent of nonprescription medicine."

Despite the fact that a very high percentage of the over-65 population have one or more chronic disorders, many of them take drugs without consulting a doctor. To lessen the danger of complications and the need for expensive treatment, care should be taken about what drugs are taken. Even over-the-counter palliatives such as aspirin can be dangerous if combined with certain other drugs.

The FDA directive will not become law until 1993. But don't wait for that. Ask your doctor to explain each medication: how they're supposed to work; what foods, drinks and other medicines or activities to avoid while taking them; what the side effects are and what to do if they occur. And ask your pharmacist if there is any indication in your prescription history that could cause problems.

You and your prospective spouse should have this information about each other, as well as be aware of your total medical regimens: drugs taken and why, diet restrictions, activity restrictions, etc.

Are both of you properly insured?

The price the nation's older citizens pay for longer and more productive lives is the high cost of medical care. To avoid the dissipation of life savings, it is necessary to be properly insured.

Medicare-age persons are covered by that government insurance, but it pays only part of the bill. Under the Medicare program, allowable fees are set by the government for each type of examination or treatment. Then, only 80% of that amount is paid.

Unless you are covered by supplemental insurance through an employer or individual policy, you could find yourself in a financial bind because of a prolonged illness or major surgery.

Supplementary policies, too, usually pay 80% of

the balance due after Medicare pays. So, even though most of the bills are paid, you will be responsible for some part of the cost. In addition, Medicare does not pay for medications. Some insurance companies do. Check out their coverage before signing on.

If either or both of you are working for a company that offers medical insurance under a blanket policy, examine the benefits and choose the best one. There have been many changes in employer-based health insurance lately, with higher costs imposed on older workers, so read the small print carefully. Weigh the costs and types of coverage. Choose the best policy for you.

Don't pay for two when one will do. That is a common mistake and a waste of money. Although that may happen when both parties work for separate companies offering health coverage, it is a more common occurrence in the community of retirees. They pay for duplicated coverage but can collect from only one company.

Under a new law, signed by President Bush in November 1990, it is illegal for any carrier to sell you duplicating coverage. If you're not certain about what you have and what additional insurance is being offered, bring your contract for Medigap insurance to your local Social Security office for advice.

Also, under the same federal law, Medigap insurance has been revamped and simplified by the

National Association of Insurance Commissioners.

The new provisions reduce to nine the number of policies now available from the maze of thousands of variations that left people confused and reeling with indecision. The basic benefits (choice #1) would apply to all purchasers; other benefits could be included in your coverage within the parameters of the eight additional policy choices.

When all the details are worked out and put into effect, it is expected that premiums for these Medigap policies will coincide with present rates: $40 to $100 per month, governed by the person's age and choice of benefits.

Although some of the new policies will cover home health care, and Medicare pays a limited amount toward care in a skilled nursing home, there can be a very large gap between actual costs and insurance payments.

Even for people who like to believe it will never happen, there could come a day when they are confronted by the medical nightmare: the unexpected need for short- or long-term skilled convalescent care. Although you may not have to go to a nursing facility, the bills for physical therapists, nurses, etc., to come to your home could gnaw away at savings.

Medicare covers only about 2% of nursing care costs. But a number of reliable companies offer insurance against such contingencies. They offer a variety of choices: how soon do you want benefits to start? How much per diem coverage do you desire (remember, nursing home costs can be extremely high)? Do you want home health care benefits?

Whether or not you are old enough to qualify for Medicare, and thus Medigap insurance, when you are shopping for health insurance, investigate the programs offered by two or three companies. Make certain the policy is guaranteed renewable for life as long as you pay the premiums, that there is no reduction of benefits because of age, and that mental illness caused by an organic problem or Alzheimer's disease is covered. And insist on a waiver of premium after 90 days as long as nursing home benefits are being paid for that spell of illness. Choose the options you want, and before you sign anything, consult your lawyer if you don't understand the language.

Don't forego travel because of a health problem.

Some people are venturesome. Others may hesitate to even consider travel because of a physical ailment. Don't think you have to be in good health to enjoy the excitement and joys of traveling near or far.

You'd be surprised how accommodating plane, train and shipping companies can be. If you have special diet requirements, use a wheelchair, are blind or have another disability, be sure your transportation company knows in advance. Although most companies have facilities to ease your way, not all are available on every piece of equipment.

For instance, some ships are happy to accommodate passengers in wheelchairs but others might have doorways too narrow for them. There are tour buses with special lifts; others are not accessible for people who can't climb up that big step.

Some Amtrak trains are especially equipped for the disabled. A man I know required thrice-weekly dialysis but it didn't stop him from traveling with his wife from California to Maryland. Amtrak reserved the special compartment for disabled and arranged a stop overnight in Chicago for a prearranged appointment at a clinic. Next day they boarded another train that took them to Baltimore and a proper care facility.

The woman who required dialysis, mentioned earlier in this chapter, took a trip to Japan, with stops along the way for her treatments.

Even cruises, which some people consider the best of all vacations, are not out of bounds for dialysis patients. There are two hurdles. The first is finding a cruise ship professionally staffed and equipped to administer the procedure. Secondly, it is expensive. The charge — about $400 for each dialysis — will not be reimbursed by Medicare. However, some Medigap insurers will pick up a portion of the fee.

Any trip for a dialysis patient must be planned well

in advance of the date of departure. Cruises are no exception. The clinic where the patient receives regular treatments may have information for dialysis on board. If not, arrangements can be made through Dialysis at Sea Cruises. Write to them at 611 Barry Place, Indian Rocks Beach, FL 34635; or phone (800) 544-7604.

Several years ago aboard a China cruise with my husband, I found that about 75% of the passengers were over 65. Many of them had one ailment or another, but everyone was active and happy. One couple, both in their 80s, was particularly noteworthy. He was nearly blind; she couldn't hear. But they didn't let either problem cramp their style. The year before they had visited Peru and ventured up the mountain to Machu Pichu. The next trip on their agenda was a cross-country bus tour of the United States.

One of our traveling companions on a Nile cruise was a woman in a wheelchair. Although she could not climb into one of the main tourist attractions, the Egyptian burial tombs, we were all delighted to describe what we'd seen and her friend took rolls and rolls of film for a reprise when they returned home.

An 80-year-old rather portly gentleman on a cruise of the Greek Islands managed to clamber over ancient ruins from Delos to Rhodes. Sometimes he was pushed and pulled to attain a special vantage point, but nothing deterred him. And back on board, he was ready to sip his martini and enjoy dinner.

So don't hesitate to follow your dreams. Do not let your health needs keep you from remarrying because you fear being a stay-at-home will make you a burden. Or perhaps your intended spouse has special needs that need not preclude travel. If you enjoy travel and all the blessings, fun and education that it offers, keep right on doing it. You'll probably feel better than if you stayed at home and only dreamt about what you'd really like to do. Certainly the adventures will be a morale booster. Just notify the carrier of your special needs, pack your bags, and go.

AIDS is a medical reality of the 1990s.

It might seem anomalous, completely out of place, that a book about remarriage in the over-50 generation should address the problem of AIDS (acquired immune deficiency syndrome). But the reality of this scourge that has swept the country (and a good part of the world) has to be recognized.

It is not a disease that chooses its victims from one segment of the population (as too many people believe). It is not confined to drug users with contaminated needles. It does not discriminate according to sexual orientation, social status, ethnic background or age. AIDS is indiscriminate about whom and where it strikes.

The sad truth is that it has crept into the older,

heterosexual population and too few people (even doctors specializing in geriatric medicine) recognize its presence.

The insidious HIV virus (the cause of AIDS) might be acquired through a blood transfusion and remain dormant for years. It was not until after 1986 that adequate testing for it became routine. Even now, however, there may be some blood sources that have not been properly tested. Many hospitals are doing their own double checking now. But it is too late for some hapless victims.

Even if a couple has been monogamous, the disease that was transmitted through a blood transfusion might unwittingly have been passed to the spouse through sexual intercourse. Some people (even doctors) forget that sex can be a joyful experience well into the 60s and 70s and sometimes even into the 80s. So, if someone has had a blood transfusion within the past seven years, testing is a highly recommended precautionary step.

It is also recommended for anyone who has had sexual encounters after widowhood or divorce.

Unfortunately, there has not been much research on the prevalence of the disease in the older population, but according to an article in *The New York Times* (11-26-90), data from the Federal Center for Disease Control in Atlanta showed that more than 10% of the 150,000 total reported cases up to that time were among the over-50 population.

The center also reported a marked increase in the

disease among women. Even though the data do not indicate how many of the women were in the over-50 age group, the mere fact that 11% of the total reported cases are women should be a signal to all women to be cautious.

New York City is particularly aware of the problem of AIDS in older people. It conducts meetings at senior citizen centers to update sex education for older persons. But New York seems to be one of the very few cities in the country to raise the awareness of the over-50s to the danger.

Dr. William Adler, chief of the National Institute on Aging, studied the progress of the disease in 45 patients 60 or older at the John Hopkins Clinic for HIV-infected individuals. One of the things he and his colleagues found was the problems involved in using the powerful drugs prescribed to treat the AIDS virus when the patients were already taking drugs for other maladies. The medications could interact adversely and even have a negative effect on the other disease(s).

Indications are that AIDS progresses faster in older bodies and the afflictions are more severe. Diagnosis is delayed for at least two reasons: first, the presumption that older persons are not sexually active; secondly, the similarity between symptoms like muscle weakness, rashes, coughs, or forgetfulness that may relate to aging but might also indicate a presence of the HIV virus. Because of the similarities, there is the possibility that AIDS symptoms may be diagnosed in the elderly as Alzheimer's.

Living will and durable power of attorney

How many times has one heard, or uttered, the words: "I wouldn't want to be kept alive as a vegetable"? But how many persons realize they can control their destiny?

They can do so through what are known as a living will and a durable power of attorney.

Signing such documents is as sensible as writing a will. In fact, they should be drawn by an attorney at the same time he or she is preparing your will.

Before the advent of all the "medical miracles" that keep patients alive, everyone understood the limitations of a doctor's skills. Accident, stroke, heart attack, diphtheria (does the younger generation even know what that is?), any of a myriad of causes of death were accepted with a heavy heart but the feeling of inevitability.

Now, however, people are faced with decisions about loved ones and themselves: do we accept the life-sustaining procedures that artificially support life; or do we, in the event of incurable injury, disease or illness, prefer to allow a natural death?

There have been several cases in the news over the past decade that focused attention on this paradox. Have we the strength to let our loved one die; or shall we keep him or her with us for as long as possible even in a vegetative state?

One of the most harrowing cases was that of

Nancy Cruzan, a young accident victim who existed in limbo for eight years because the courts refused to allow disconnection of life supports. Her parents went through years of pain, anger and sadness as well as innumerable suits, until finally the U.S. Supreme Court granted permission to withdraw the feeding tube that had prevented a dignified death.

Following the Supreme Court's decision in the Cruzan case, the Congress enacted a new federal law that mandates that patients who enter a federally funded hospital or nursing home must be given information about their rights under state laws to refuse treatment. Patients also are entitled to question the institutions about their practice in such cases so they can choose one that will honor their decision.

Also, institutions are required, under the Patient Self-Determination Act, to record whether the patient has a written directive (a living will or health care proxy) that will become effective immediately upon incapacitation.

The federal law relates only to federally funded institutions. It is important, therefore, to check out the practice regarding directives in private institutions you might consider using.

More than 40 states have living will laws, but some of the documents drawn under those laws can be vague. New York State does not have such a law, but, like 17 other states, allows health care proxies. But such designees may hesitate to make decisions.

To be able to specify your own wishes, have your attorney prepare documents according to your state laws. However, care should be taken that all contingencies are covered. The more precise you can be, the better for all concerned.

A medical directive prepared by Dr. Linda Emanuel and Dr. Ezekiel Emanuel sets forth the pertinent information. It may be obtained for $1 and a stamped, self-addressed envelope (and reproduced for personal use) from the Harvard Medical School Health Letter, 164 Longwood Avenue, Fourth Floor, Boston, MA 02115. It covers four possibilities — persistent vegetative state, coma with a chance of recovery, dementia and dementia with terminal illness — and offers a choice of specific responses.

Summing up ...

Once again, ideas have been offered in this chapter that may seem too down-to-earth when you're walking on air in anticipation of a new life. But it does take a dose of realism *before* marriage to enhance what is to come.

Health may play an important role in the marital relationship. Being pragmatic about sharing information will inform both of you about everyday regimens and may make it easier to handle medical emergencies if they occur.

CHAPTER 6 RELIGION AND INTERMARRIAGE

Do religious differences pose a problem?

We are fortunate to live in a country where society usually does not accept or reject a person because of religious practices.

Schools, universities, businesses and industry may request this information for statistical records, but under Federal law, it cannot be used as a deterrent to advancement. Admittedly, the law sometimes is ignored.

Even though many social and cultural organizations are ethnic, religious and color blind, acceptance is not always assured, even in this enlightened age.

When it comes to marriage, there continues to be objection — sometimes strongly expressed — to allowing a "stranger" into the family circle. This is more likely to occur when younger people are involved rather than with seniors.

Some parents find it impossible to swerve from their position against intermarriage. They try to influence young adult children to abandon the relationship. Sometimes they are successful. But in today's climate of independence, they don't always win. If they fail, wise parents compromise to avoid estrangement.

The withholding of family approval does not happen often when the man and woman who are marrying are in their middle or later years. They have a different relationship with their parents (if the parents are still living) than do younger persons. They have been in control of their own lives for too many years for parents to influence their decisions. Parents may express regrets but have little power to change minds.

There might be other family members — sisters, brothers, even cousins — who are not pleased about the marriage plans. That may happen if there is orthodoxy or rigid belief in the tenets of their religion.

Sometimes even adult children of the couple might object. Most often, though, children's objections are not based on religious differences. In fact, they themselves may have married out of their faith. (See *Chapter 9* for other objections of children.)

Nevertheless, just as in any marriage, when older people remarry, they marry a family as well as a new mate, and the atmosphere is far more pleasant if there is acceptance all around.

Gaining friendly acceptance of intermarriage is becoming easier because of changes in attitude within the churches and synagogues.

In the wake of a liberal movement toward reconciliation in houses of worship, many denominations have eased their stance about intermarriage and are welcoming mixed couples to religious services as well as educational and social activities.

One of the dilemmas that has to be resolved by younger couples is not a consideration when the people involved in the intermarriage are older. That is the question of religious upbringing for the children. For the person remarrying in the middle years or later, any children involved are already grown, or have reached their teens and are already getting a religious education of the parents' choice. It is natural for them to continue the path already directed and accepted.

People marrying someone of a different religion usually welcome an opportunity to expand their knowledge and enrich their lives. They read and sometimes take courses offered by churches, synagogues or local colleges. When they have a better understanding of the history and rituals of the religion, they find they are comfortable attending even the most solemn services regardless of denomination.

Doris said that Sunday church service is important to her. She confessed that, although she was brought up in a strict Catholic home, she doesn't feel very religious. On the other hand, she feels Sunday isn't Sunday unless she goes to Mass. Sometimes Bob goes with her. He is a nonpracticing Jew, but she was interested in his heritage, so under the direction of the local librarian, she did a lot of reading on the subject. Now, she says, she knows more about it than he does.

Margaret, too, was raised in the Catholic church and still attends Mass. She also goes to temple with Louis during the High Holy Days. She finds the prayers and rituals beautiful and inspiring.

There are a growing number of intermarriages in this country, and each couple has to reach its own reconciliation of the differences.

For people who are nonreligious, there is no difficulty. But when one or both of them feel a need to attend services and follow their own religion, the problem is not insurmountable. It is important to work it out before the marriage.

Differences in religious beliefs are not as acute in older marriages except where there is rigidity. In that case, it is wise to explore the subject very carefully in advance of the marriage to avoid friction in the marriage that could exacerbate other differences.

In *Building a Successful Marriage*, the Landises remark on the positive approach to a mixed marriage: "The person with a positive religious faith that impels him to behave ... according to a standard based on respect for others and acceptance [of others] ... is more likely to be capable of satisfactory relationships with others and hence [is] a better risk as a marriage partner."

The person whose faith has a strong base will have the flexibility to understand the other person's viewpoint. Thus each will be able to honor the other's point of view.

CHAPTER 7 THE TWO-CAREER MARRIAGE

The two-career marriage is not unique in today's world. It has been with us for several decades, especially among the young-marrieds.

But more and more, with the change of law that abolished mandated retirement at age 65, people are continuing to work well into their 70s and even into their 80s. This is true of long-marrieds, singles and remarrieds. Some persons who had retired are picking up the strands of previous careers or initiating new interests to improve their financial situations or to keep their lives vital and interesting.

Men used to work until their 65th birthdays, when retirement was decreed because of company policy or because the idea of the leisurely life beckoned. Often the siren call to a life of golf, tennis and breakfast with the boys evolved into a routine that induced ennui or restlessness — a desire for the stimulation found in the structure and activity of the business world.

Sometimes, even though the easy life was pleasant, it was prudent to go back to work because inflation had gnawed away at the nest egg. In either case, they opted to re-enter the job market in the area of their expertise or in an entirely different enterprise.

Women who worked at the usual female careers of the prefeminist era — nursing, teaching, secretarial, sales — also were bound by the same age 65 retirement injunction.

However, many women in their later years returned to work after the children went off on their own, or circumstances forced them back into the commercial milieu when they were widowed or divorced. Still others who had never worked outside the home went back to school to earn degrees in a chosen discipline, or to become licensed in particular occupations. During the 1970s and 1980s real estate was a popular choice for women pursuing new careers that allow a flexible work schedule.

Two careers in a marriage can enhance and stimulate the relationship if each of the parties is willing to make certain adjustments to work schedules, social activities and household duties.

Attitudes and adjustments of some working couples

Becky is a community relations director at a radio station in a large mid-western city. Her husband is a businessman. She is in her late 50s; he in his early 60s. Although her radio programs are heard mornings, taping sessions are arranged to accommodate visiting professionals in many fields — social work, medicine, literature, arts, politics. In addition, there are luncheon and evening meetings associated with her work and with the considerable charitable work in which she and her husband Louis are engaged.

About sharing the household chores, Becky remarked: "We exercise parity when appropriate. Louis's job keeps us afloat (local radio is notorious for low pay). Each of us does what must be done in understanding and encouragement."

Louis feels sharing household duties, even for Becky's low pay, is worth it because "her job enhances our scholarship."

A couple of years after Molly and Jim married, she began to look for a career that would stimulate her and be financially rewarding. After a couple of fits and starts she opened her own art gallery, which is a successful enterprise. Jim said he was "in favor of her business fully."

Molly spoke more about Jim's work. "He shares as much [household duties] as possible, but he works 12- to 14-hour days. We're both pleased with his job. The demands on him are many, but he loves the challenge and responsibility. And we're both happy about his job and the activities and travel it includes."

Several years later, however, the atmosphere between them changed. Jim felt she had abandoned him when he lost his job. There was no understanding or empathy, he thought. That and other compelling factors led them to the divorce court.

Evelyn, aged 68, and John, 78 at the time of their marriage, worked out a satisfactory arrangement. She had her own business, a telephone answering and secretarial service; he was semi-retired. "He worked part-time," she said. "It's good therapy for him and it leaves him time for me and friends. And it's nice that he helps with the house."

Felice admitted: "We have two different business philosophies." They have a business partnership dating from the early days of their 19-year marriage. At the time of our first interview in 1982, they owned one restaurant and he managed another at a large sports establishment. "His job at the other facility was very demanding, and I felt left out sometimes. We talked about it. Eventually I adjusted. As for household chores, I have help and we eat out a lot."

Although their marriage ended in divorce seven years before my final contact with her for this study, they continue their business partnership (they now own three restaurants). They remain on friendly terms and continue to dine together occasionally.

Certain adjustments by Cathy and Bill were necessary, but each was happy to accommodate to assure a compatible marriage. She told me: "I am a part-time working wife, and my husband is very considerate and protective of me. He does not care to help too much at mealtimes and prefers that we eat out. He is very helpful and considerate in our home, and we have part-time cleaning help.

"His occupation (as a state official) is very demanding of him and me. However, there are tremendous benefits, particularly his personal growth, which makes my contributions very worthwhile and pleasurable. His work brings out the best in both of us."

"Her job," Bill conceded, "may interfere at times. However, my wife is a mature individual who has to have a responsible position to challenge her mind. I commend her for her ability to have a variety of interests and still be a good wife, mother, daughter and friend."

There's a different perspective about a working relationship as expressed by Carol and Tom. She says: "He thinks he shares, but not really. I changed my profession [from human resources and organizational development to real estate appraiser] because he was obsessed with his work [real estate appraiser], and it seemed like a good way to share. It has worked out well. Although we have the same profession, we are involved in different markets. I sometimes resent his interference, or what seems to me interference, in my expertise."

Tom said: "We share outside/inside [household] work; we have and enjoy independent and communal life." As for their work: "We help each other over the rough spots of the job. [There is] no conflict."

For several months Fred, a Ph.D., went through a transitional period. He was collecting unemployment compensation while trying to decide on a new career. He'd been a sociology professor at a large mid-western university. He had become disenchanted because of the administrative tasks connected with his work, and he hated the politics he believed were permeating his academic world.

Ellen, who worked full time as a teacher, reported that he was taking care of their small daughter except for four hours a day when the child was at a neighbor's. Fred was doing all the cleaning and laundry, plus cooking three evening meals a week. Said Ellen: "Knowing he was with our child was a psychological help. His help with the chores was wonderful. We've had much time together — neither of us looks forward to his having to return to a nine-to-five workday."

Unhappily for that marriage, Fred eventually chose to buy and operate a large truck, hauling loads interstate. It took several years, but eventually his preoccupation with his work and long weeks of separation while he was on the road led to disintegration of the marriage.

This is only a small sample of how working couples deal with the interdependence and compromises required to make a congenial union. Sometimes they work out very well; sometimes not.

CHAPTER 8 FINANCIAL SECURITY, WILLS AND PRE- OR POSTNUPTIAL AGREEMENTS

"I hope you will have a place in your book on the working of finances for older couples who each have children," Janice urged. "And something about making financial plans beforehand when one of the couple has more than the other."

It is my hope that this chapter will give Janice and persons on the verge of remarriage some guidance in those and other financial preparations to avoid disputes and possible tax complications.

Whether or not you are considering remarriage, if you are a once-married with only a few assets, you should have some inkling about how to handle those assets and the best way for you to make your holdings grow or produce income if that is what you need.

Even if you think you know nothing about the securities markets, or municipal bonds, or banking, you can learn. Every town has brokerage firms that offer public seminars; some have schools that offer adult education courses on investments. Take advantage of whatever opportunities are available.

Don't expect to become expert. At least you will be able to speak intelligently with your banker or broker about how to handle your assets.

Your public library has a variety of books about how to evaluate your financial situation and others that give suggestions for budgeting, investing and otherwise controlling your assets. Several are listed in this book's bibliography. One of the most informative and instructive is Dorlene V. Shane's *Finances After 50.*

Shane points out that with life expectancy (1989 statistics) at age 71 for men and 78 for women, there are a growing number of questions, especially for those in the upper age brackets: how to maintain physical, emotional and financial health; what to do about increasing health costs and possible diminishing income. *Finances After 50* discusses prudent money management, inflation and the changing tax picture.

The book offers ideas and step-by-step planning tools for individuals and couples who are (or are planning to be) married:

- Planning for retirement.
- Figuring your projected incomes and how much each will contribute for regular expenses and planned holidays or major purchases such as cars, appliances, etc., and how to estimate your needs.

There are recommendations for different ways of getting the best financial deal if you own a home:

- Sale leaseback to family or other investor with a guaranteed lifetime lease. You receive the proceeds either as a lump sum or monthly income; the purchaser pays taxes, maintenance, upkeep, etc.

- Reverse mortgage. This is a monthly loan advance (from a bank, mortgage company, other purchaser) for a fixed number of years or as long as you live. The loan usually is based upon 60-to-80% of the appraised value of the property.

- Line of credit reverse mortgage. The homeowner chooses when and how much of the loan advance to take to cope with unexpected costs.

- Home equity loan or second mortgage up to 80% of your equity in the house.

Understanding yourself and your financial needs and expectations may not necessarily equate with your spouse's positions on those matters. You may have to compromise when the two of you are not on the same plane. That is why discussion leading to prenuptial agreement is advisable.

There was a time not too many years ago when the suggestion that a couple planning marriage should sign a prenuptial agreement was considered an unfriendly act. It kindled hurt feelings and occasionally cancelled the anticipated wedding. But things have changed, even among the age group that used to shudder at the thought — those born before the early 1940s. With the increase in the divorce rate among all age groups over the past 15 or 20 years, the greater affluence of people over 50 and all the ancillary factors involved, more and more people are seeing the wisdom of such a plan.

You may be one of a dwindling number of people who are put off by the term *prenuptial agreement*; you may equate it only with the financial arrangements a wealthy man makes with his young wife-to-be so the idea, to you, may seem crass. But the old-fashioned connotation is misleading.

Prenuptial contract (or understanding, if you prefer) signifies an intelligent approach to marriage, especially for older individuals each with children or other responsibilities. It can mean the difference between success or failure of the marriage.

Family counselors report that money is a more frequent cause of marital difficulties than is discord over child-rearing, lifestyles or other friction points. That holds true regardless of the spouses' ages, the length of the marriage, or whether it is a first marriage or remarriage. It is reason enough to find out where you both stand regarding planning, sharing and arranging for the use of your resources during your lifetime and disposition of your estates when the time comes.

Sensible planning and legal steps taken before the wedding bells ring will give each of you, and your children, confidence that this new marriage will not be plagued by money problems. These steps (financial planning, prenuptial agreement and the signing of wills) will free each of you from the anxiety of "What will happen if ... ?"

When one party has more assets than the other, the use of and eventual disposition of them will be prearranged in accordance with each individual's desire and the agreement of the other person. Then each will be reassured about the future disposition of the estates and how the money will be apportioned for their daily needs.

Such pragmatism might seem to be a dash of icy water to someone in the lovely haze of a new love. But that old cliché, "Better to be safe than sorry," makes a lot of sense.

However, if you hesitate to broach the matter before the marriage or if there is a change in your holdings (perhaps you've bought a home together, made a large purchase of securities, inherited), all is not lost. Once you have settled into a pleasant connubial routine, you might decide that you do want to proceed with legal steps to correct or enhance your financial arrangements. The agreement you reach and the document your attorney draws is called a postnuptial agreement. It has the same legal status and requires the same input as a prenuptial one.

Understand the need for prenuptial agreements and financial planning.

The financial arrangements you make before embarking on a second marriage (or after vows have been exchanged) probably will be different from your earlier marriage. Many persons who married during the first half of this century had different concepts of the roles of husband and wife.

It was not uncommon for the man to take care of all the finances — except perhaps for his wife's control of the household allowance. That is why too many women are left in a quandary about insurance, checking accounts, wills, Social Security, mortgages and the myriad money matters that are a part of living.

However, we cannot always blame the morés, the era, or the husband when a woman is ignorant of the family's finances. There are many women like Lillian Ross, whom I interviewed for my previous book, *About Mourning.* She was a working woman with a good salary. Except for personal needs or whims, her income was deposited to their joint accounts. She was unconcerned, almost indifferent, about how their money was spent or invested. Lillian believed her husband would always be there to take care of her and their children and she didn't want to hear about their finances.

A lot of women who fit into the "didn't want to know" category have had to learn the hard way following the loss of their mates. Even if they have not become financial wizards, they have at least mastered the rudiments of balancing a checkbook and stretching income to pay the bills. Lillian found it difficult but necessity forced her to learn.

Now that ideas have changed regarding mutuality in marriage, whether the simplest transaction gives you grief or you believe you're a financial wizard, marriage counselors agree it is important for both of you to put your ideas about money management into words and work out your differences before the marriage.

"At his request," Doris remarked, "I take care of the finances. This is a natural for me in view of my accounting background. One thing I learned, however, is that he is a comparison shopper and I'm not. If I want it, I buy it. Period! Fortunately we are both well off financially so can't foresee problems in this area. Time will tell." It worked out fine for them. The marriage was a very happy one that lasted 11 years until Bob's death.

Of course, not all couples talk over money matters before they marry. Even so, for some it works out very well despite warnings to the contrary.

Fred said: "We pooled our incomes with the exception of her holdings from her previous spouse. These go to her children."

Steve and Edith did not discuss finances before their marriage, but, said Steve, "... things sort of fell into place. We have our own incomes so no money worries. We had no special plan but Edith took over some of our expenses, I others. If I pay most of the big bills, she saves more of her money for both of us."

Edith teased him about his "male chauvinism." "He thought he should pay all the bills. But I have a pension and Social Security [payments] so we've worked out a plan for each to pay certain things."

Another thing they shared is their household furnishings. Edith moved into Steve's house, which they had started to renovate before the marriage. But she retained ownership of her own home. "I have a friend who signed a premarital agreement because her new husband wanted to make certain the home they were sharing would go to his son when he died. If he died before my friend, she would be in a dilemma about where to live. For that reason I've kept my house and have it rented out. So if Steve dies before me, the house will go to his children and I'll have a comfortable place to move into. Meanwhile, the rent I collect is very nice."

More frequently, though, couples are being pragmatic about prenuptial agreements.

Bill told me: "I was aware people would say Cathy was getting a good thing by marrying me, but it wasn't like that at all. If she married me for my money, she signed away all of it in our premarital agreement. I told her frankly I believe half of everything I had was Goldie's [first wife] and really belonged to our children. Cathy didn't question it at all. I'll probably make changes from time to time. You know," he admitted, "you have a feeling maybe the marriage won't work out and you want to protect the children. You may feel like a youngster emotionally, but I was 58, she was 52. Your ideas are pretty well set and you wonder if it's going to work. At least I did. And I didn't want to take that step without thinking about that. Now it's three years and I know I was worried about nothing."

Bill pays all the bills, but Cathy does the household bookkeeping, and they talk over investments for each of their accounts. Also, Cathy continued to work. "I love my job and I don't know what I'd do with myself if I stopped, although I have cut down from five to three days a week. Besides, I don't think I want to give up that feeling of independence. With apologies to my dear Bill, I like the feeling I don't have to go to him for everything. It's not that he's not generous — he's a dear — it's just, well, I've been on my own for so many years."

Plan your finances.

There is no reason for anyone to feel threatened by the reasonable suggestion that you sit down together to define your marriage with your heads as well as your hearts. Analyze honestly your financial situations and plan your future. This is the same process you followed when you were determining whether or not you were ready for the big step (remarriage), and if so, had you chosen your new mate well.

If the idea of revealing financial worth and planning together is repulsed, there must be something wrong with the relationship and you should step warily before you go forward with the wedding plans.

Unless you already have a list of all your assets, you have been remiss. Even if you think you don't have "all that much," you'd be surprised. You may discover you are worth more than you realized.

Laying out a financial plan allows you to exercise your options about what happens to your holdings — financial and personal property — if the marriage fails or when the time comes to dispose of your estate.

This is a reality that some people stubbornly refuse to face. Nevertheless, it must be confronted. It is far better to confront these matters now rather than later under duress.

To begin, each of you can prepare a list of your holdings: savings, real estate, securities, life insurance, personal property such as art or antiques, pensions, annuities, Social Security income, etc. Then make a list of your mandated obligations: mortgages, taxes, insurance, alimony or child support payments, loans, car payments, etc. Figure the net worth of each of you.

Your bank or your accountant can supply personal financial statement forms which may help you to organize your information.

Make notes about which assets will be a part of your marriage. For instance, if, like Steve and Edith and many others, each of you owns a home, will you keep both, live in one and rent out the other?

Or will you sell one or both before the marriage to take advantage of the tax break for persons over 55, then buy a new house? There are tax considerations in each case which will be discussed later.

Other facets of financial planning are decisions to be made regarding children, living trusts, annuities, and contributions to the joint financing of your marriage.

All these matters can be worked out between you and set down in a premarital agreement drawn by an attorney or in mutually exchanged letters. However, you should be aware that, in many states, there are limits on the acceptability of such letters in probate courts and divorce courts, if that event were to occur.

When either or both of you have more than very modest assets, it is sensible to consult a financial advisor and your attorneys. They will help you work out the most propitious arrangement.

Before consulting attorneys and financial planners, your own children should be told privately about your individual financial status and your plans to arrange to safeguard your assets and their interests in them. This will reassure them that they are being protected. The openness could convert your children's possible negative attitudes about your marriage to pleasure that you will be happy and your life more fulfilling.

After you have listed your assets and advised your adult children of your plans, then it the time to approach a financial planner if you don't have one already. These tips will help you select one:

- Consult your CPA. He or she may be the most qualified person to recommend a financial planner. Look for a Certified Financial Planner, who has met stringent course requirements, a qualifying examination, and must have ongoing education. The Institute of Certified Financial Planners, 1-800-282-PLAN, will give you a list of certified practitioners in your area. Financial advisors sometimes have a product to sell (insurance, securities, or other kinds of investments). Depending on your personal ideas and needs, that could pose a conflict of interest, so consider that aspect carefully.

- You may also ask your friends, attorney and banker for recommendations.

- Ask to see plans developed by the financial planner for other persons; study them carefully to determine if they fit the pattern you want established.

- After you make your choice, get references from at least three of the planner's longtime clients.

- Make certain you understand the planner's fee schedule. Will this be a one-time plan with perhaps only a review every few years? Or will you want an ongoing relationship with the planner giving you advice on asset sales or purchases? In the latter case, what will be the basis for fees?

- Have the planner present a complete written plan. Also, keep notes of conversations in person or by phone.
- Review the plan with a critical eye. Do you feel comfortable with all aspects of it? Does it reflect your expectations and address your needs?

Plan your estate.

Conventional estate planning is reasonably simple for a first-time marriage. In most cases husbands and wives draw simple wills leaving everything to the spouse, even when there are minor children. The general belief is that the surviving parent will take care of the children's needs while they are young.

When the children are grown and self-sufficient, it is surmised that the surviving spouse probably will need the assets for his or her support and retirement.

In the case of remarriage, when there are children from a previous marriage, leaving everything to the spouse can leave children from an earlier marriage out in the cold.

Therefore, before the wills or prenuptial agreements are made, to avoid discontent or anger, a family conference is an imperative. It should include all the children (and, if they exist, grandchildren) old enough to understand such matters.

Even if all the interested parties are aware of plans for the eventual disposition of your holdings, there is always the possibility of hurt feelings and even anger.

At the time the will is signed, circumstances may suggest unequal bequests. For instance, if adult children are self-sufficient they would have less need than younger children still in school or just embarking on a career. To avoid hostility or sensitivity, the legator could attach a letter addressed to each of the heirs that would express the parent's love for the child and explain the reasons for the uneven apportionment. The personal letter from parent to child could also be a good way to bequeath personal property or special gifts.

However, children grow up, financial security can erode, or other situations develop that would change what one considered an equitable arrangement written into the original will. If the parent is anxious to be fair to all heirs, it is very important to keep in mind the changes taking place in the lives of the heirs. Legal experts recommend a re-examination of wills at least every five years; more often if circumstances warrant.

Philip Roth, in his book *Patrimony* in which he describes his relationship with his father, was surprised by his reaction when his father told him he would not receive any bequest. "But now with his death anything but remote, being told by him that he had gone ahead and, *on the basis of my request* (italics added), substantially eliminated me as one of his heirs elicited an unforeseen response: *I felt repudiated* (italics added) — and the fact that his eliminating me from the will had been my own doing did not at all mitigate this feeling of having been cast out by him ... my bedrock feelings were sometimes more conventional than my sense of unswerving moral imperative."

There may be any number of situations that can lead to disruption of the family. One that occurs frequently is when an older man marries a younger woman — maybe the same age or even younger than his first family. That may be a prescription for real nastiness if there's a family business in which the older children work. Suddenly they may find the stepmother in control even though she has never shown any interest in the business.

This unhappy event can be avoided by setting up a trust that makes certain everyone is provided for. One type of trust is a QTIP (qualified terminable interest property) which gives a percentage of net income from a business to the spouse. Upon the spouse's death, the property passes to the children. No estate taxes are due on the property until the death of the remaining spouse.

In setting up a QTIP, one must take great care when selecting a trustee. The person should be an unbiased administrator favoring neither the spouse nor the children. After all, the children wouldn't want the spouse as trustee, second guessing every business decision. Nor does the stepparent want to be totally dependent on the children.

With an impartial trustee, the trust would be managed without prejudice toward any party, and presumably, to everyone's satisfaction.

In addition, with everyone's monetary share dependent upon net income, the children would be encouraged to run the business efficiently and strive for greater profits. It would also assure the stepparent of a reasonable regular income.

Different problems may arise if the father and young wife have children together and no provision has been made for his older family to share in his estate.

Included in the prenuptial decision about estate planning is whether or not children of a former marriage should be adopted by the new stepparent.

In the case of divorce, that cannot be done legally without written conset of the noncustodial parent. If there is no such signed agreement and the custodial parent dies, custody will revert to the surviving biological parent. That is not always the happiest solution. In cases where there is a dispute between the biological parent and the stepparent, the court will decide custody. Usually the biological parent is given custody when the children are under the age of 14. However, in these cases, the judge usually talks privately with the children and makes the decision based on what is in their best interests.

Legal advice should be sought early in the marriage to prepare for this possible unexpected contingency and avoid the trauma a court hearing might impose on the children.

Still another question to be considered is whether each party to the marriage wants to provide only for his or her own children, or do they want to include stepchildren? If the stepparent wants to make certain provision for a well-loved child of the spouse, it can be done through trusts or other financial devices.

These are only a few of the factors to be considered when consulting with your CPA, financial planner and attorneys. (I use the word attorneys rather than the singular, because most consultants believe the interests of each party to the contract are better served by separate representations, at least in the premarital discussions.)

Each estate plan is tailored to the needs and desires of the individual, or couple. It is based on the financial holdings of each party to the marriage and their relationship to each other and to their families. It also is subject to change as children grow up, lifestyles change and the financial outlook improves or deteriorates. So it is important that, whatever legal steps and financial arrangements are set before or after a marriage, they should be re-examined at least every five years.

Other financial puzzles: the pension plan and alimony payments

One facet of financial planning that is not thoroughly understood — or is ignored — is the pension plan(s) that is being counted on as part of regular income.

In some instances, the person collecting a deceased spouse's pension may become ineligible for that income if she or he remarries. When a person retires, the terms of the company pension should be completely understood. Don't depend on the company's explanation. Show the plan prospectus to your CPA or attorney.

The General Accounting Office (GAO), the investigative arm of the U.S. Congress, issued a report in late 1990 that may signal trouble ahead for some pensioners. The GAO cautioned that the law that is supposed to ensure pension benefits to a surviving spouse may not be offering the protection intended.

The consent forms signed by pensioners and spouses when the form of retirement benefit is chosen do not always clearly delineate all the options; or the forms are not always written in understandable language. They are filled with legalese that may be confusing.

Under Federal regulations there are crucial facts the employers are not required to include. Some forms do not make clear that continuing the pension after the death of the pensioner (the so-called joint and survivor option) means lower payments during the lifetime of the insured. Nor do they explain that opting for the single-life annuity which pays maximum benefits to the retiree, means the surviving spouse will receive nothing.

Although the Internal Revenue Service is looking into the GAO's recommendations for changes, don't wait for implementation. And don't ask only the employer for explanations. Show the forms to your CPA or lawyer before you sign anything.

If your spouse had selected a choice of payment form at an earlier time, he or she can sign a new form that will change the pension arrangement to a more suitable plan to fit the marital needs.

Susan hesitates to make a commitment because she fears cessation of the income she receives under the terms of her deceased husband's pension plan. "What if the new marriage doesn't work?" she worries. "I'd have no income because I'm still not eligible for Social Security payments. Besides, I didn't earn enough during my working years for that to pay me very much."

Alimony payments are another type of income that may be jeopardized by remarriage.

One couple delayed their marriage for many years until her children reached the age of 18 and the large alimony payments ended. This was in the 1950s, a time when women often were granted substantial alimony.

Today's courts are looking for more efficacious financial arrangements in divorce cases.

In addition, under existing tax laws, it probably is best to accept child support payments rather than lump sum or monthly alimony. If you're in the process or facing the possibility, consult with your CPA before a final ruling is made by the court.

Legal aspects of a prenuptial contract

Is a contract necessary? Does it help? Most people think so. But there are some who don't.

Let's look at the negatives first.

Some lawyers are of the opinion that prenuptial contracts protect the wealthier partner, often to the detriment of the other. To protect the assets of the more affluent, the spouse has to give up certain marital rights.

There are various state laws that govern "equitable distribution" of property in the event of divorce. Without a prenuptial contract, the spouse (usually the woman) will be granted 30 to 50 percent of the marital property. When an enforceable contract has been signed, the contract will control the amount of property to which each spouse is entitled.

Some attorneys are cautious about the conflict that may arise when the subject of prenuptial contract is raised before a marriage. That is a time when love and belief in the future envelop the couple. Those feelings may be crushed when the subject is raised. That is especially so for anyone who fears that including provision for divorce in a premarital contract can be a self-fulfilling prophecy. There is no indication that statistics exist to confirm or deny that superstition. But overcoming it can put a pall on the marriage plans.

However, if the marriage is consummated merely for what one can get by ending it, someone has been the victim of a vulture worse than those described in an earlier chapter.

There do not have to be unhappy feelings over a prenuptial contract.

First of all, such a contract, as previously pointed out, does not indicate distrust. What it can do is strengthen the relationship because all the cards are on the table and the marriage begins in an atmosphere of honesty and trust.

Confronting the *possible* points of discord before they pop up at an inappropriate time allows for negotiation before a crisis arises. That is why legal advisors emphasize the importance of separate attorneys. In fact, failure to have independent representation for the drawing of a pre- or postnuptial contract will vitiate the legal effect of the agreement.

The prenuptial contract under discussion here is to protect the assets (personal, real estate, savings and other holdings) that each party brings to the marriage and those accumulated or spent during the marriage. It has nothing to do with a simple exchange of letters or other written or oral agreement that plans (particularly when both spouses work) division of household and parenting responsibilities, vacation and other individual preferences.

Those are beyond the law. They are private decisions between the two persons. If you feel better about putting these ideas in writing for your mutual benefits (as many younger career couples are doing), you can sign them and they may be recorded but they would have no status in a court or probate proceeding.

Earlier, it was suggested that you each consult with your own attorney about financial and other provisions to be included in a prenuptial agreement. The final contract will be drawn by one of them in consultation with the other.

There are specific provisions that can be a part of the documents you sign that will protect the financial rights of each. Most states will accept an agreement signed by both parties. Notarization or acknowledgment are not necessary in California and maybe not in other states. But the court may nullify a prenuptial contract if it includes arrangements for compensation in the event of divorce (or if there are other stipulations that may adversely affect the spouse's interest) unless an agreement has been signed by the spouse.

Under the "Uniform Premarital Agreement Act" in California (effective January 1, 1986), such a stipulation is regarded as encouraging divorce and is consequently illegal. The law in your state may have other nullifying restrictions.

For instance, in some states if one of the parties to the contract has failed to give full disclosure of assets and their value, the court might consider the contract null and void.

Pre- or postnuptial agreements must be carefully drawn to conform to the laws of your state. They must be realistically planned and structured to fit the needs and values of the parties. Those are requirements that only an attorney knowledgeable about the law can incorporate into the contract.

The purpose of the pact is to define each one's expectations, rights and responsibilities after marriage with regard to separately owned property, jointly owned property, joint purchases, division of joint living expenses, child custody and support, disposition of property in the event of the death of either spouse or other dissolution of the marriage. etc.

Because these are complicated matters and the laws of the states vary, professional expertise is essential.

Some of the things you should be prepared to discuss with your attorneys are:

- The rights and obligations of each in any property of either or both of you. The respective rights of each party to the property owned by the other at the date of marriage, and the proceeds of sale and/or refinancing of such property, and the income derived therefrom.

- The rights of either or both of you to buy, sell, use, or otherwise manage and control the property.

- The rights of each party in property acquired after marriage, and the proceeds of sale and/or refinancing of such property, and the income derived therefrom.
- The disposition of property upon death, separation or divorce.
- Executing a will, trust and other documents to carry out the provisions of the prenuptial agreement.
- Ownership rights in and disposition of the death benefits from life insurance. The rights of each party in the vested retirement benefits of the other and of any contributions to such benefits made subsequent to the marriage.
- Provision for such matters as those of place of abode, freedom to pursue career opportunities, child rearing, disposition of property to his/her/their children, mediation of marital disputes.
- Any other matter either of you or your attorneys may consider important.

Legal aspects of the postnuptial contract

Postnuptial contracts are signed for a variety of reasons. Even couples who have been married a long time may decide to sign an agreement because of changes in finances, business and family status. For those recently married, where there was no prenuptial signing — regardless of the reason —

the couple may have decided the timing is right.

They may reach a mutual decision that a clarification of property ownership is necessary to clearly define the status of inherited property; or they may want to simplify future questions of division of property in case of death or divorce. (Beware! An improper phrase could invalidate the document.)

For tax reasons, the couple might want to change community property to joint tenancy, or vice versa.

A word of caution: transmittal of real or personal property signed after 1984 is not valid unless it is written, accepted and signed by the spouse whose interest is adversely affected.

Another tax consideration: the transmuted property may be subject to gift or estate tax. If the gift is subject to restrictions on the spouse's use, it may not be subject to gift taxes. However, the gift might be subject to estate taxes on the death of the spouse.

To repeat a previously stated precaution, both parties should be separately represented. If, for some reason, they are not, the attorney drafting the postnuptial contract must point out possible conflicts of interest, if they exist, and obtain written consent of both parties.

The intricacies and laws of the various states that govern these matters can be sorted out only by professionals in the field who are concerned with the best interest of their clients. That is why the importance of separate attorneys is emphasized.

The steps you will take preliminary to consulting your attorneys are the same as if you had executed a prenuptial agreement.

First, consult your CPA or financial advisor and reach some kind of consensus about your aims and the contingencies you want covered. Then discuss all the facets with your attorneys.

Taxes and the remarried couple

Although you may have reached agreement about how you expect to finance your marriage (how the bills will be paid, your savings plans, how you will invest income, etc.), there is another important area that should be discussed with your CPA. The man or woman who prepares your income tax return can offer advice that could reduce your tax obligations.

One of the first things to be decided, if either or both of you own homes, is whether to sell or rent the house(s), buy a new home or condominium or rent.

The IRS allows a once-in-a-lifetime tax exemption on the profit from the sale of a house up to $125,000. To qualify for the exemption, you must have passed your 55th birthday and you must have lived in the house three out of the past five years. In order for both spouses to obtain the benefit, each must complete the sale of his or her house *before* the marriage.

One couple in my study (like many others, I'm

sure) delayed their marriage for several months until her home was sold so she could take advantage of that opportunity to enhance her personal financial situation.

If the bride and groom each owns a home, they may decide both should be sold and a new home purchased — perhaps with the proceeds from both sales. Any surplus would remain in their separate accounts.

Those two words are very important to remember: *separate accounts.* In the event of death of one of the spouses, or divorce, there should be clear and concise records about what assets each person held before the marriage and their value, the appreciation, income and expenditures connected with those holdings — whether real estate, securities, savings or other assets. The lack of such records could result in one big tangled mess to straighten out with the IRS, the state taxing agency and the heirs of each spouse with regard to income and inheritance taxes and ownership rights.

During the marriage, the appreciation and income from individually owned property in some states is considered part of the marital property and is taxable as such. In some states any property acquired during the marriage is considered marital property. There are certain exceptions that allow ownership to be joint tenancy. Your attorney can clarify the law for you.

Marital property is held either as community

property, co-tenancy property or joint tenancy property. Joint tenancy property passes to the surviving joint tenant automatically upon the death of either joint tenant, and the decedent's will or estate plan will have no impact on that property.

However, spouses in community property states can *create* substantial income tax liabilities upon the death of either spouse if appreciated or appreciating property is held as joint tenants. This is where the advice of an expert in property and tax law is essential to avoid the adverse financial possibilities.

In the event, however, that one of the couple wants his or her share of the property to go to a child or other heir, ownership should be switched to community property.

There are additional intricacies to be discussed with your CPA and attorney.

Consider the incomes you both will receive from Social Security, pensions, annuities. These are partly or fully taxable. While IRA and Keogh accounts are not taxable, withdrawals from them are. At age 70½ one must, under the law, withdraw a certain sum annually from either of those savings plans. The mandated amount is based upon IRS actuarial tables based on the ages of both persons.

There are certain kinds of trusts that can be set up to give you income and avoid probate.

One is a *revocable or living trust.* This allows you to have full use of the property (a house to live in, for instance, or the ability to buy and sell the securities in the trust). You will pay taxes only on the earnings. This type of trust will not impact on your income taxes; it will avoid probate, protect your assets and leave you with the option to withdraw any or all of them at any time. Your estate will pay taxes on the assets in the event of your death.

An *irrevocable trust* may reduce income and/or estate taxes. It may incur gift taxes. You have no control over the handling of the assets. While you may believe, at the time you set up the trust, that the income will be sufficient for your future needs, inflation, illness, or changes in life style might dictate greater need but there is nothing you can do to change the trust.

Whether your holdings are sizable or modest, there are things you can do to reduce the impact of income or estate taxes. Consultation with CPA, financial advisor and attorneys regarding investments, wills, and prenuptial agreements will ease the emotional and tax impact on you and your new spouse, and, if there are children, stepfamilies.

Legal and tax ramifications for LTAs (living-together arrangements)

In an earlier chapter, there was discussion about couples who, for whatever reason, choose to live together without marriage. There is nothing unique about that arrangement even among older persons. Marriage is an ultimate commitment that some individuals cannot make. That doesn't necessarily indicate weakness. Whether a couple is married or in an LTA, how they relate to each other can make their lives a celebration if their finances are discussed and arranged before the involvement is solidified.

There are certain financial and legal realities that many in an LTA are not aware of or choose to ignore. There may come a time, when either because of the death of one or a decision to separate, a web of tax questions and legalities can evolve into an entangling web. This is most likely if the couple has mingled income or bought a house, furnishings, car, etc. together.

Just as meticulous record keeping is suggested earlier in this chapter for remarrying couples, so it is for LTAs. If one pays for a sofa and another the bedroom set, each with his or her own money, hang on to that check or Mastercard slip. If a house is bought together, some states consider it community property and it may be considered such by the IRS and the courts. If each brings certain assets to the relationship, there must be proof of ownership. If there is a pooling of funds, it makes good sense to lay down rules about contributions and expenditures, and keep records.

Consultation with attorneys and CPAs (even when the sums involved are modest) about how to manage finances, assets and large purchases is as important for LTAs as it is for couples who choose marriage. Perusing this entire chapter will give an indication of how to prepare for the conference.

Signing an agreement similar to a prenuptial contract, and being sensitive to possible areas of discord, will make the LTA relationship easier both emotionally and legally.

CHAPTER 9

THE REMARRIED FAMILY

Stepfamilies are a mass phenomenon.

"Today the stepfamily is a mass phenomenon involving 35 million people as stepparents and stepchildren," said Dr. Clifford J. Sager, the director of family psychiatry for the New York Jewish Board of Family and Children Services. His words are taken from an article in the *New York Times* on January 4, 1979. Statistics have changed very little in the intervening years.

It was about that time — 20 years or so ago — family therapist Virginia Satir originated the term "blended family" to designate the new entity that emerges from the marriage of two people, either or both of whom have children from a previous marriage.

That appellation always bothered me. Somehow, when I hear "blended family," my mind conjures a silly picture of someone with a big spoon stirring together ingredients to concoct a new product. In a way, I guess that's exactly what happens when a man and woman who have children wed and merge families. But I prefer to call them exactly what they are — a *remarried family*.

They are individuals — mothers, fathers, children,

stepmothers, stepfathers, step-siblings — each with specific personalties, who will develop new relationships and bring different perspectives to the new reality. These will be complex relationships. To a great extent, the outcome will depend on the man and woman who will head the household. It will take patience and understanding by each of them before and after the ceremony. The importance of dialogue is incalculable between the biological parent and the stepparent, then each with his or her own children, and, finally, the man and woman with all the children.

One can barely comprehend the multifarious intricacies and problems of new relationships when so large a number of persons, each with his or her own uniqueness, is involved. What each is looking for is guidance to solace them through the maze of conflicting emotions and experiences.

Professionals in the fields of family and child services agree that problems will arise regardless of how understanding parents and stepparents try to be. The intelligent approach to helping two families become one means adequate preparation of everyone involved. There are several steps that will lay the groundwork for integrating two families with a diversity of needs and desires; to make the merger a treasure chest of love and understanding with as few tribulations as possible, instead of a Pandora's box of problems.

Pietropinto and Simenauer (see *Preface*) point out

that remarrieds "seemed to quarrel more over children because of the complex problems that arise in mixing full-, half-, and step-siblings." An intelligent approach is preparation beforehand.

The first step, of course, is telling your children your plans, giving them an opportunity to meet the new person who will be part of their lives (if they haven't already met), and involving them (especially younger children) in wedding preparations. It is best for each child to be told by his or her own parent.

Announcing the news to adult children is less likely to produce conflict or negative feelings. Nevertheless, there will be some adult children who will be unhappy about the idea. Unhappy or not, it is not their place to tell a parent what he or she can do.

Gail Sheehy points out in *Pathfinders* that adult children have a "responsibility to listen and empathize." She states further that they must accept the individuality of the parent and his or her right to make decisions that won't necessarily please the child's self-indulgence.

When a divorced parent is remarrying, if the children are young — even into their early teens — it destroys their dream of a reconciliation by their "real" parents and a return to the family that had been. This can make the children angry and destructive to the new relationship.

Those who remarry when there are preteen or teenaged children may be confronted by problems that could be eased with proper preparation of every member of the family.

Remarriage when there are adult children

When someone is considering remarriage, the ideal, of course, is for everyone — including all adult children of both the bride and the groom — to be delighted when Mom or Dad announces intentions to wed.

Sixty-nine-year-old Paul looked like a kid with a special secret as he sipped tea in the sunny kitchen of his daughter's home. "I want your permission to marry Ina," he said, hesitating before each word. "I didn't believe that someone my age could ever feel this way — I thought the sex urge was long dead, but I've learned it's not."

"But of course," his daughter grinned. "Why did you even think you needed our permission? And who but old wives ever said sex stops at a certain birthday? We know how lonely you've been since Mother died and I'm delighted you and Ina have gotten together. I've known her almost as long as I can remember, and I think it's wonderful, and I'm certain the rest of the family will agree with me."

Those who remarry in midlife or later and become stepparents of grown children will be pleased to realize, as Ina did when she married Paul, that their lives are enriched by the newly acquired children. They find they have gained young adult friends without the demands that are imposed by child rearing.

When the relationship between parent and adult children has been reasonably open, friendly and understanding, announcement of marriage plans is an occasion for rejoicing.

Bert reported joyously: "Ruth and I were married last July with a wedding party consisting of 25 siblings ..."

Steve and Edith talked about how their children — his two and her one — would react to their announcement, but they weren't worried. He knew his daughter had been concerned about him and was certain — and his surmise proved true — that she would want to see him remarried and happy. He had always been close to his son and was not disappointed when Steve, Jr. concurred with his sister's view.

Edith's son and stepdaughter (both her first and second husbands had died) were equally pleased when they learned of the wedding plans.

Oddly, the one person Steve and Edith were worried about was his mother. She was the one who thought it was "terrible" that he was dating. The mother had lived alone for 60 years following her husband's death and "I guess that's what [she thought] I should do," Steve said. "Somehow she felt it was disloyal to contemplate remarriage — or even date someone. We kept putting off having her meet Edith, but finally decided we had to face her."

Steve had told Edith about his mother's love of

gardening and growing house plants, so they arrived with a very special variety of violet "all done up with pretty ribbons." The gift provided the perfect opening for their conversation and the two women discovered they had both been school teachers and had other common interests. "In the end, my 91-year-old mother conceded, 'I guess it isn't good for somebody to live alone,' " Steve chortled.

Marie said: "My boys seemed pleased when we told them. George's kids said, 'So soon?'[after their mother's death]. But they also were happy about it."

Of course it wasn't as easy as that sounds. Marie and George sought counseling before the marriage to try to avoid possible problems. Even though his children accepted — in fact, were quite pleased — with the marriage, it was important for the parents to take control so there would be no question of where the line is drawn between the child's rights as an individual and obligations to the family and society.

Although Marie's and George's children were all grown — aged 21 through 27 — two lived at home; two were away at college but came home for vacations and summers; and the 27-year-old was a frequent visitor.

"With five children, friends, cars, etc.," Marie pointed out, "we pretty much called the shots. We purchased a large house so everyone had their own bedroom and privacy. But we could see where we would go crazy if we didn't rule the roost. We were the only parents that didn't allow drinking; no boy- or girl-friend visitors if we weren't home; house kept neat; chores done; etc., etc."

Marie admits it wasn't all wine and roses in their combined household. "There are always problems that come up. We eventually work them out. I think we all realize we will never have a true parent-child relationship and don't expect it."

She continued: "Children establish their habits, personalities and peculiarities by their teens. His children run against my grain — mine, his — at times. You can't change them, only tolerate them. Our main problem is that I can't be honest and vent my problems with his kids [when I get angry at them] but then, finally, I blow up and the truth comes out."

The positive response of adult children in these cases is not always duplicated in others. Some grown children — whether they are married or not, but especially those who are unmarried and still living at home — may be angry and resentful.

Helene Arnstein suggests in her book, *Getting Along With Your Adult Children*, that the idea of a new husband or wife sleeping in the same bed their parents once shared may be repugnant. This leads to the feeling that the parent's remarriage is an act of disloyalty to a deceased parent. It actually is the opposite. Remarriage, when a person has been widowed, is actually a paean to the deceased. Persons who have *enjoyed* the institution of marriage will, once the loss of a beloved mate has been integrated, want to seek the comfort and companionship of another. It is illogical for an adult child to act so immaturely, but if that is the reaction, the parent, and possibly the new spouse, will have to handle the negative, angry feelings with understanding and diplomacy.

"We have to realize our kids can be difficult at times," Bill told me. "My daughter, who is married and lives in another city, voiced no objections about my dating *several* women, but when I told her about plans to marry, she made it clear she didn't want anybody [permanent] in my life."

Bill's daughter, whose feelings about Cathy were complicated by unresolved bitterness and guilt over her relationship with her deceased mother, learned that warmth and friendliness were a good basis for forming a relationship with her father's wife.

Bill said: "We had the benefit of grown children out of the city which can be an advantage in the formulative years of a second marriage."

He continued his description of the evolution of the new family and how his daughter finally realized her fear of being shut out was unfounded. "Our relationship had always been very close and special, and she was afraid she'd have to share me. At first she tried to ignore the fact of the marriage. She was cool when she met Cathy, but began to change when she herself became pregnant. She was impressed by the fact that Cathy had the interest and took the time to buy a layette. Now she tells me, 'You're lucky to have someone like Cathy to be with you.'

"As for my son, there was never any problem there," Bill continued. "He's more communicative, warmer, and he was open to Cathy's outgoing personality. He saw that she made me happy and felt glad about that."

Cathy's report indicated a rosier view of their early days together: "During the time we were dating, we both met each other's children. All of our children were cautious and watched their parent. There was sufficient time so that nice relationships were formed — and these relationships have improved and mellowed during the years of our marriage."

There was an extra bonus for Bill when they married. He became a ready-made grandfather of Cathy's year-old grandson. That really excited him. Then the bonuses multiplied for both of them as both his and her children began to add more grandchildren to the family circle. By the time Bill reached his 72nd birthday and Cathy her 65th, some of the grandchildren had reached their teens. It is now, literally, one big happy family. It's no longer "your grandchild" or "my grandchild." It is "our grandchildren" and two delighted grandparents traveling from one city to another — or welcoming the children into their own home — to savor the joys of grandparenting.

Ronnie's concern was with her daughters' attitudes: "The first year was very difficult. It took almost that long to resolve any conflicts with my daughters and for them to accept the idea that I was going to marry the man. I lived with him in *my* home. They had moved out to their own apartment. We did [eventually] reconcile and went on with our own lives." But there were complications with his 15-year-old son. "The boy lived with us for about two years until he left home ... [my husband] let me know that he would discipline, handle his son. I was not to be anything but a warm, caring stepmother. I tried to do as he wanted. Eventually he [the son] dropped out of school — went back to his mother for awhile and lived with others. There has been an off-again-on-again relationship with his father all his life." The son is now in his 30s.

Alice and Fred found mixed reactions from their children. He reported: "I told mine as soon as I had asked her to marry me. I believe hers just seemed to know it before they were told of its certainty. My meeting her children the first time was great. I liked them both immediately."

Although all their children except his 19-year-old son were on their own, there were objections. "My children are estranged from us," Fred continued. "They are not happy about my remarriage," he acknowledged without rancor. "Her children are both married, one living in our city, the other in another state. We see both their families often and communicate by phone at least once a week."

Alice was sad about the estrangement between Fred's children and their parent. "My spouse's son, after our marriage, was constantly in debt. After many loans and his unwillingness to work, Fred turned him down when he wanted a sizable amount of money. He has never spoken to his father since then.

"Regarding Fred's daughter," Alice went on, "we brought her to live with us three years after we were married. She was in high school and got into drugs after two years. I was not able to cope with the situation and she was placed in a private home. She is now married and my husband sees her regularly. I do at family gatherings."

Those were the negative reactions. But, she commented: "My older son was delighted since he was getting married. My younger son, still in high school, ignored us. It was difficult at first," Alice admitted. "My young son was the only one at home in our early years of marriage before he went to college. [But] in those first three years my husband became my son's confidant, more so than I and it has increased tremendously with both my boys. [Fred's] relationship with my children and grandchildren is beautiful, if possible, more beautiful than mine."

One of the oddities that can crop up with adult children and new spouses is the question, "What do

I call her (or him)?" It is understandable when an adult cannot use the very personal term of Mother or Dad. But some are so reluctant about accepting the stepparent they even have a problem addressing them as "Jane" or "John" instead of "Mr." or "Mrs. Jones."

In the end, each person, or couple, has to confront the crises as well as possible under existing circumstances. But it is helpful to turn to the knowledge and sagacity of persons who have studied the human psyche.

Martin Buber's wisdom has guided many persons in their search for understanding of themselves and their ability to relate to others. When a mature couple is considering how their marriage will affect their relationships with their adult children, they and their children should consider his words:

"The best cooperative relationships are not those in which we attempt to win each other over to our own ways of seeing things and to our own satisfaction; they are the relationships in which we try to understand and respect the other person's self."

Informing preteen and teenaged children

Once a decision for marriage has been made, informing the younger children should be high on the priority list of things to be done.

Each child should be prepared by his or her own parent. It is easier if the children have met and spent time with the prospective stepparent. However, it is far different for a child to enjoy being with Mama's friend than to think of that person as becoming part of the family. So don't expect miracles when the children meet the future new parent after digesting the news.

If each of the parties has children, the next step is for them to meet and be given an opportunity to learn a bit about each other through conversation and activities.

Then it is time for the entire group to sit down and reason together. This holds true whether the children will be living with you or the other parent (in cases of divorce and special custody arrangements).

The ideal would be if everyone knew and liked everyone else. That rarely happens. But even when there is no previous acquaintance, warm, friendly and open attitudes by the parents (and the other, divorced, parents) can pave the way to eventual good relationships all around.

The remarried family with prepubescent or teenaged children

Some of the problems that confront younger families will be of little concern to the mature men and women at whom this book is aimed. Nevertheless, that word "mature" encompasses a wide age range — from about 45 upward. And at the younger end of the scale, it is possible (as seen in several of the cases cited in this chapter) that there will be teenagers or preteens involved in the remarried family. Therefore, it is important to consider the ramifications and be prepared to work together to seek solutions. Parents or stepparents who are rigid foster that same attitude in the children. When that happens, none of them learns the dynamics of give and take that are so necessary for working out compromises.

The adults can set good patterns of behavior by really listening to what the children have to say and being flexible in their own judgments and pronouncements.

Even the eminent Dr. Benjamin Spock, whose books were the "bible" on child rearing for several generations of young parents, entered unknown territory when he remarried at the age of 73. Along with a new mate, he acquired an 11-year-old stepdaughter.

"I found I didn't know beans about being a stepparent," he admits in *Spock on Spock*. "I'd no idea how painful it is to feel rejected by someone within the family or how hard it is to respond rationally to this." He finally sought professional help to understand the child's and his attitudes in order to bring about a warm relationship between them. It took several years.

One of the lessons Dr. Spock learned — the hard way — was that no matter how much the stepparent might be suffering, the child probably is suffering more.

There is little doubt that remarriages are most complex where there are prepubescent and teenaged children. At that age they are struggling with the normal physical and emotional vicissitudes of their years. There is a certain amount of hostility in kids during the transition period. They want independence, not control.

E. Mavis Hetherinton, University of Virginia psychologist who studied a large number of stepfamilies over a period of many years, recommends acting like a polite stranger. Be warm, responsive and communicative. Monitor the children's activities without demanding unquestioning obedience.

That may be sound advice, but it seems like an oversimplified response to very complex circumstances.

"Establishing a marriage relationship *and* a parent relationship at the same time is extremely difficult because you are adjusting to a whole family relationship ..." June and William Noble, in *How to Live With Other People's Children*, quote psychologist Margaret Doren's astute description of the difficulties inherent in a remarriage where there are children.

Emma said: "I think the word stepparent should be erased from our vocabulary."

But the word is there to stay. It is the connotation of the fairy tale "wicked" stepmother that is negative. It should be eliminated. In the majority of remarriages Cinderella's stepmother is a fiction that can be relegated to the wastebasket. Most men and women work very hard at being good stepparents. What they need is some guidance, encouragement and the opportunity to work out the problems.

The founders of the Stepfamily Association, a national network with chapters in many cities, decided to be direct and use the dreaded appellation, because, as Dr. Emily Vishu said to a *New York Times* interviewer in 1983: "If you dance around a word you never change its connotation ... only by repeated use [of the word] in a more positive light would we change the image."

"The most important thing that makes a stepfamily work," Dr. Doren continued, "is for the two adults to love each other enormously. they must put each other first and then work out the problems with the stepchildren. Whenever the stepchildren are placed first, above the stepparent, the marriage is in trouble."

Felice admitted that her children were happy about the marriage, and his seemed to be, but: "I don't feel they've ever truly accepted me. I feel I've never been allowed to have a relationship with them."

The same dichotomy existed in Joyce's marriage. "His relationship with my 13- and 16-year-old sons was good; mine with his 16-year-old daughter was strained due to her mother's negative influence. It was all ironed out eventually."

Emma conceded her daughter was frightened by

Alan after seeing him in a manic attack. "She was the only one of the children who lived with us. She did not like [him] and was not happy about the marriage. However, she tried to adjust by avoiding [him] as much as possible. I believe it contributed to her early marriage." Emma's son usually likes everyone, so even though he knew Alan was manic-depressive, he reacted positively. The boy's father had been killed a couple of years earlier in the crash of a commercial airliner and "he wanted and needed a father very badly."

Anyone who has parented children during those crucial years — 11 through 17 or 18 — knows the kids really spend very little time with their birth parents, let alone sharing time with a stepparent. So don't take offense when they refuse your offer of a game of tennis or a trip to the pizza joint. They'd rather go with their friends.

Add the complexities of bringing an interloper into their milieu and situations may arise that will call for hard adjustments by each person involved.

The intricacies and textures of the family bond are influenced by family experiences and an atmosphere of acceptance (or lack of it) within the family circle. So it pays to invest the time and energy for comprehensive examination of relationships involving all the interested parties before the wedding and the creation of the new family.

Teenagers are in the process of debonding, taking tentative steps toward full independence from their parents. But they continue to need the assurance that the family and the love are always there in the background. Although they are seeking and developing new relationships outside the family, they want them to be of *their* choice. They may be angry or resentful of new relationships thrust upon them — including an unexpected and unwanted stepparent. Sometimes, therefore, the normal emotional vacillation from self-confidence, even arrogance, to insecurity during that time may be heightened when confronted with a new parent, and possibly stepsiblings.

How parents react to this up-and-down behavior pattern will determine the stability of family relationships.

Dr. William Mitchell and Dr. Charles Paull Conn in their book, *The Power of Positive Parenting*, suggest the use of Dale Carnegie's primary rule: good communication is when you talk less and listen more. That's a bit of wisdom we could all abide by.

Dialogue is so important — an exchange of ideas, not just talking *at* each other as if there are two separate monologues.

Despite your determination to 'do it right,' if you are ready to throw up your hands or feel you are about to erupt in anger and frustration over your own or a stepchild's actions as he or she explodes into puberty, take heart — and give some thought to consulting a family counselor.

But before you turn to professional help, read the

four-page introduction to Jean and Veryl Rosenbaum's *Living with Teenagers*. You might be consoled by their words and try to work out the problems within the family. The information is a revelation on teenage behavior extremes and the mature persons who emerged from their individual maelstroms.

In fact, that entire book is worth reading for its down-to-earth, intelligent guidance for anyone who has teenagers at home. In 1980, when their book was published, the authors had a combined 40 years of clinical practice with teenagers and parents. That invaluable experience is evident in the "special empathy" they have for teenagers' "unique struggles."

"If you use common sense in parenting," the Rosenbaums conclude their introduction to the book, "the years of living with teenagers are later rewarded by mutual commitments of unconditional love and care."

Stepparenting is, indeed, a complex and sometimes confusing predicament for even the most intelligent, patient, discerning adult. There are many, many books by experts in the field of human development covering countless aspects of this special task which sometimes seems easy and at other times hopeless. Some of those books are listed in the bibliography.

I encourage you to pursue additional study or consultation with experts in the field if the problems of stepparenting seem insurmountable. After all, if the noted Dr. Benjamin Spock admitted he needed professional help, certainly no one else should shrink from the idea.

The family conference: defining the rules of behavior

When children of either or both spouses become members of the new household, many complicated and unforeseen circumstances arise and may be aggravated by the natural debonding process of teenaged emotional growth. Because of the numerous possibilities for negative emotions, substantive education and planning involving the adults and the children are necessary to encourage harmony. The education and planning are vital whether the youngsters will be living with the newlyweds or will be "visiting" children who come for weekends, holidays and summertime.

The noncustodial parent can encourage the child to integrate into the group without disrupting his or her own parental connection. To maintain the emotional link, the "part-time" parent can keep in contact through frequent letters and phone calls between visits.

Unless explicit guidelines and rules are agreed upon beforehand, there may never be an opportunity for friendship and compatibility to develop. Quite the contrary, associations may be marred by erroneous preconceptions, misunderstandings, jealousies or conflicting loyalties.

Early reluctance and ambivalence on the part of children, especially teenagers, is natural. It will take love, patience, a foundation of exchanges of ideas and expectations, and setting behavioral ground rules before trust will displace suspicion. Don't expect utopia. If you do, you're in for a rude awakening. Remember, even in "original" families there are bound to be some dissensions. Don't plan on an argument-free household. If you do, you'll be disappointed and maybe disheartened.

Before the marriage, arrange a meeting — or several, if that seems advisable — of the parent, prospective stepparent and all the children. Do it in a pleasant setting with plenty of time for everyone to voice feelings and concerns. The children may be wary of that invitation to openness. It will be the parents' responsibility to assure them that you sincerely want each child to participate.

The conversation should have no subtleties. Everyone must be fully aware of the meaning of every sentence. Talk about love and patience and each one's feelings about discipline, authority, rules and regulations. Make it clear that part of growing up is learning to handle negative emotions and developing skills for dealing with them. That is why you are placing such strong emphasis on the family conference as an integral part of your lives. It will be the way to prevent minor grievances from escalating into warfare.

Underscore the fact that if everyone cooperates, the amalgam offers the opportunity for a good life for everyone.

Admit that you know there will be hurt feelings and tears when altercations arise because of criticism, jealousy, anger, misunderstandings, etc.

To lessen the children's uncertainty, a plan can be set forth (prearranged by the adults and open to discussion) to become operative immediately upon setting up the new household. A specific time and place for family conferences can be established. Provision can be made to allow anyone with a legitimate concern or question to request an unscheduled meeting. But the convener must give everyone enough notice so personal calendars can be adjusted. It doesn't matter if the choice for regular (or special) meetings is Saturday mornings or Tuesdays after dinner, as long as it is convenient for all and each person understands that, except for an emergency, everyone in the household (including any "part time" available child) is to participate.

After everyone has become acquainted and fairly comfortable with each other, an early meeting should be called. This will be for the parents to set out rules of behavior — chores to be done, rooms to be kept neat, clothes hung up, homework schedules, curfews, permissible behavior with friends in or out of the house, allowances, driving privileges, etc.

At the meeting the children will have the right to

ask for explanations and possible changes. But once the regulations are laid down, everyone will be expected to comply.

This forum will permit creative thinking about all areas of the relationships, the role of each parent (biological mother/stepfather; biological father/stepmother); the relationships between them and all the children and between the national and stepsiblings.

Unfortunately, sometimes there are divorced parents who are so angry and bitter — even vengeful — their behavior interferes with the development of a good relationship between child and stepparent.

This pattern occasionally made the early years of Joyce's marriage to Robert distressing. "My relationship with his daughter was strained due to her mother's negative influence. But it was ironed out eventually."

Before such conduct exacerbates the situation, the subject should be broached and explored at a family conference. The child must not be used by the divorced parent as a conduit to inflict damage on the remarried family. The child can be encouraged to talk about it and delve into the feelings — anger, frustration, confusion — caused by the exploitation of the child's natural desire to please a parent.

Once the confab has become a regular part of family routine, perceived grievances, loving thoughts and everything in between can be aired with the certainty that there will be no recriminations for articulating complaints — only attempts to settle differences in an amicable way.

That doesn't mean there won't be arguments, anger, frustrations and jealousies. After all, this is a group of human beings, not paragons. But each person will know that negative feelings need not be swallowed. Instead, they will be listened to and solutions sought. Disagreements are normal in all relationships but children can be taught (and some adults might need reminding) that you don't always have to win an argument. Nor does anyone have to hide feelings because others may get angry with them. What is expected is that the perceived injustice will be aired in a forthright manner without name-calling, sarcasm or cruelty.

Parents of teenagers should realize that, rather than simply ordering their children around, they should become listeners, hearken to the adolescent's opinions and criticisms. That's not always easy. It means forgetting one's own sensitivity — especially if the teenager is disagreeing with you. Weigh the speaker's thoughts; show him or her respect. Ask questions that will clarify the controversy and point to solutions. The questions should be gently probing rather than acerbic. "Why do you feel like that?" "Can you tell us why you acted that way?"

The family and the individual

It is worth remembering that all relationships involve some conflict. If the adults assessed their reasons (emotional and pragmatic) for the marriage as suggested earlier in this book, they will be girded to withstand pressures that may affect the marriage relationship. The idea of talking things out between themselves will be extended to the children without fuss or furor.

The dialogues can be reassuring to the parents as well as the children. Parents might suffer guilt pangs that the remarriage brought on the children's problems and misbehavior.

The point is discounted with a breezy reality by Robert Farrar Capon in *A Second Day,* his amusing discourse on the joys and perils of remarriage:

"Childhood ... is a sea of problems anyway. Concern over whether your remarriage is responsible for creating them makes about as much sense as worrying whether your emptying a Coke bottle into the ocean contributes to the flooding in a hurricane."

Dr. Paul Bohannan, anthropologist, states the same premise in a more serious manner: stepchildren "have to face an obstacle course, but all children do; these youngsters just have a different obstacle course." (*New York Times* 1/4/79, Dullea article)

It was Capon, however, who offered a sage piece of advice. He recommended that no one be denied the right to mention the problems or complain about them. On the other hand, anyone connected with the problem or the complaint should have an opportunity for rebuttal.

"Criticism of parental systems can be easily understood if those systems are sound and workable. If the system is faulty, perhaps a teenager can offer constructive suggestions," the Rosenbaums counsel. They recommend that you keep your sense of humor, don't be defensive, reinforce the trust between yourself and the children.

Provide a home environment that, by your own behavior, encourages openness and honesty and makes it easy for a child (or one of the parents) to admit, "I made a mistake," That, probably, is one of the hardest things for anyone to say. But being able to say it can smooth away a lot of anger.

The teenagers, and the parents too, should be *allowed* to have legitimate peeves and angers. Talking about them offers opportunities to correct misconceptions.

And *don't be afraid to apologize when children express hurt feelings*, whether by words or behavior.

If candor is laced with good humor, the family conclaves can palliate hurt feelings, find solutions for some of the problems, reduce tensions and strengthen the family circle.

It is naive to expect a child to instantly bond with a stepparent. Expect overt or subtle rejection. For instance, the child may act as if the stepparent doesn't exist; or be combative about every suggestion made by the stepparent.

It takes time for children, regardless of age, to assimilate a new adult into the family structure. Even though your early conferences will set down lines of discipline and clemency, don't be too assertive. It can take as long as two years before a child will accept discipline from the stepparent. If you start the relationship by trying to chastise the youngster, he'll get his back up and damage your hope for mutual respect and cooperation. So try to relax. Let the children come to you in their own good time. In the meantime, let the biological parent deal with the sticky problems that may disrupt the household.

However, no child should be allowed to play one parent off against the other. The biological parent might over-indulge the child because of guilt feelings or if he or she is insecure in the parent-child relationship. That bias can drive a wedge between parent and stepparent.

Those decrees carry the same weight with live-in or weekend children. No child should be allowed to rule the roost. That can lead to disaster for the marriage.

Recognize that everyone needs time alone, separate from the rest of the family. You may want to set definite times and places for the desired privacy or let each person "signal" a desire for solitude when the personal need arises. This should no be difficult as long as the times chosen do not disrupt family plans or routine. After all, it would be unfair for one child to suddenly decide he needed to be alone in the middle of a serious family discussion, when he has been given chores to do, or just as the family is embarking on an outing.

Once the family meetings have covered other phases of living together, it will be time to talk about "family time," what each of you expects from it, things you'd like to do together as a whole family or in small groups.

If rules are followed, a lot of the friction burns will be soothed and the family conclaves usually will be successful.

Part of loving is understanding that everyone has certain needs, emotions and ambivalences. Learning to *Communicate, Negotiate and Compromise* is essential for strengthening the love and respect that builds good families.

Adjusting to major changes takes time — especially for the often rebellious adolescent. Each person is unique. When integrating two families with their many personalities and idiosyncrasies, don't try to fit the others into a mold that suits you.

Teach the children by example. Guide them, but don't push. Someone else's "norm" may not be yours. But maintaining your sense of humor and sense of balance, and learning to live with your own limitations and those of other persons, bodes well for your remarriage.

One final word of caution from Dr. Chaim Ginott: avoid promises. "Promises," he wrote, "should neither be made to, nor demanded of children. Life is too uncertain for promises."

CHAPTER 10 FINAL STEPS

Plan the wedding.

Alfred, Lord Tennyson may have had only one season of the year and one age group in mind when he penned the well-known:

"In the Spring a young man's fancy lightly turns to thoughts of love."

But love comes, too, to persons in their later years. And, if they think they've found a congenial, compatible person they may want to wed, they don't consult the calendar to see if it's the proper season.

Carl Jung, in an essay on *Youth and Age*, differentiated between those two stages of life: "The afternoon of life is just as full as the morning: only its meaning and purpose are different."

To be able to bring new vitality, meaning and purpose to "the afternoon" of your life through a new, close relationship is a blessing worth seeking and embracing when it happens.

If you've read this far into this book, you probably fit the profile of a mature person whose thoughts have turned to love — and not very lightly at that. You've given serious thought to the idea of remarriage; you've examined your emotions and analyzed the many facets of remarriage discussed in these pages. You have welcomed the blessing bestowed upon you. Now it's time for the final step — the wedding.

This is a time of excitement and happiness. Planning your wedding should be fun.

There was a time when two people, who had been married to others in the past, decided to join their lives, they would do it quietly. They chose a civil ceremony or a quiet church service, with or without a couple of friends as witnesses, and then notified their families and other friends.

Things have changed. Today, more and more persons remarrying in their later years find joy in gathering friends and family around them for this special occasion. It is a significant event that will change the rest of their lives and it's wonderful to enfold everyone within the circle of joy.

Inasmuch as you've taken up the option for marriage, you now can approach the happy dilemma of choosing how you want to celebrate the event.

Do you think you'd like to take a cruise and let the captain of the ship do the honors? Or find the nearest judge, minister or rabbi?

Would you like to have a small wedding with only close family gathered around you?

Or do you really want a large, gala affair with friends as well as family sharing your happiness?

The decision is up to the bride and groom. But before plans are finalized, consult your children. Even if you decide on a short ceremony at city hall or in the minister's office, your children and grandchildren, if you have them, may want to share the felicity with you.

The family consultation is most important when there are children, regardless of their ages. But where there are young, preteen or teenaged children, counselors find making them a part of the ceremony can help strengthen the new family structure. Most adult children would be delighted to give away the bride or act as best man.

But don't jump to the conclusion that all children do want to participate. Some youngsters may feel it would be disloyal to their divorced, biological parent or to the memory of a deceased parent. They may decide they would be more comfortable as a guest at the nuptials rather than a participant.

There may even be the unhappy situation in which a child adamantly refuses to attend the ceremony. This reaction is a warning signal to be dealt with immediately. If it is only a child's fear of the changes in his or her life, the parent may be able to overcome the trepidation with patience, love, and understanding. If that doesn't work, then professional help is important — the sooner the better for all concerned.

Adolescents are struggling with the complex transition from childhood to adulthood. It is not easy for them to accept that their parents are sexual when they are just beginning to confront their own sexuality.

The teenager's sex may influence his or her reaction. Usually when parents get divorced, daughters tend to handle it better than sons. When parents remarry, the opposite occurs: sons seem to deal with it more easily than their sisters.

In the case of a divorce, the daughter still has her strongest parental relationship: mother-daughter. But when the mother remarries, the daughter may feel she's losing her to someone else.

In fact, if the situation is not confronted before the marriage, that sense of loss could taint future family relationships.

After all the uneasiness and fears are put to rest, then it's time to invite the children, and grandchildren if any, to participate in creating the plans for a gala occasion. A 5-year-old grandchild would delight in the role of ringbearer; a teenager who sings in the church choir or plays a musical instrument might be very pleased if invited to perform during the ceremony or reception. Your eagerness for the children to take part in planning the event could generate enthusiasm and ideas for making the wedding very special.

It would present an opportunity to involve all the children from both sides of the aisle. More importantly, it could be a giant step toward a successful integration of the remarried family.

Being a part of such an important happening, whether as a participant or guest, may reassure the children that they are not being forgotten, that they truly are a part of a newly enlarged family.

If the party will include your friends, you could suggest that the children in the two families also could invite a friend or two. Having a close friend invited would make them feel more comfortable and more sanguine about your thoughtfulness and concern for their well-being.

Now the time has come to select the site, make reservations, choose your flowers, choose a caterer (if it's to be a large affair), and perform all the other things one must do to have a glorious wedding day. This book will not help you with those selections. There are many books, wedding consultants and other sources to turn to.

"... the art of life is the most distinguished and rarest of all the arts," wrote Carl Jung.

It is my hope that you have gained a bit of the expertise it takes to practice successfully, and with happiness, "the art of life."

BIBLIOGRAPHY

California Legal Forms and Transaction Guide, March 1990, Cumulative Supplement 19, Matthew Bender, Times Mirror Books.

Statistical Abstract of the United States, 1990.

Summary of California Law, 9th edition, Volume 11, by B.E. Wilkin, San Francisco Bar, Bancroft-Whitney Co.

Tax Aspects of Marital Dissolution, Harold G. Wren, Leon Gabinet, David Clayton Carrad; Callaghan & Company, Deerfield, IL, October 1989.

***

Ackerman, Paul and Murray Kappelman, M.D. *Signals - What Your Child is Really Telling You.* New York: The Dial Press/James Wade. 1978.

Arnstein, Helene. *Getting Along with Your Grown-up Children.* Philadelphia and New York: M. Evans and Company, Inc./J.B. Lippincott. 1970.

Brentbard, Stanley H. and Clarence, Sammons, Donna. *The Price Waterhouse Book of Personal Financial Planning.* Henry Holt and Company. 1988.

Buber, Martin. *I and Thou* (new translation by Walter Kaufman). New York: Charles Scribner's and Sons. 1970.

Caine, Lynn. *Widow.* New York: William Morrow. 1974.

Capen, Robert Farrar. *A Second Day - Reflections on Remarriage.* New York: William Morrow. 1980.

Chapman, Dr. A.H. *Parents Talking, Kids Talking.* New York: J.P. Putman Sons. 1979.

Dahl, Gerald L. *Everybody Needs Somebody Sometime.* Nashville: Thomas Nelson. 1980.

Derlega, Valerian J. *Sharing Intimacy, What We Reveal To Others and Why.* New Jersey: Prentice Hall. 1975.

Dinkmeyer, Dan Sr. and McKay, Gary D. *Parenting Teenagers—Systematic Training for Effective Parenting (S.T.E.P.).* Revised.. New York: Random House. 1990.

Duberman, Lucille. *The Reconstituted Family, A Study of Remarried Couples and Their Children.* Chicago: Nelson Hall, 1975.

Einstein, Elizabeth. *The Stepfamily: Living, Loving and Learning.* New York: MacMillan. 1982.

Epstein, Joseph. *Divorced in America.* New York: E.P. Dutton. 1974.

Erikson, Erik. *Childhood and Society.* New York: W.W. Norton. 1950.

Fassler, Joan. *Helping Children Cope, Mastering Stress Through Books and Stories.* New York: The Free Press/MacMillan. 1978.

Fraiberg, Selma. *Every Child's Birthright: In Defense of Mothering.* New York: Basic Books. 1977.

Freud, Anna and Solnit, Albert. *Beyond the Best Interests of the Child.* New York: The Free Press. 1973.

Friedan, Betty. *The Second Stage.* New York: Summit Books, 1981.

Friedlander, Saul. *When Memory Comes.* New York: Farrar Strauss Giroux. 1979.

Fromm, Erich. *The Art of Loving.* New York: Harper and Row. 1956.

Furman, Erna. *A Child's Parent Dies.* New Haven: Yale University Press. 1980.

Gardner, Richard A., M.D. *The Boys and Girls Book About Stepfamilies.* New York: Bantam Books. 1982.

Gaylin, Willard, M.D.. *Feelings, Our Vital Signs.* New York: Harper and Row. 1979.

Gehrke, S. and Kirschenbaum, M. *Survival Patterns in Family Conjoint Therapy —Myth and Reality.* Family Service Agency of Marin County, CA.

Ginott, Dr. Chaim. *Between Parent and Child.* New York: MacMillan. 1965.

Grinstein, Alexander, M.D. and Sterba, Edith, Ph.D. *Understanding Your Family.* New York: Random House. 1957

Guarendi, Dr. Ray. *Back to the Family*. New York: Random House/Villard Books. 1990.

Harris, Louis. *Inside America*. New York: Vintage Press. 1987.

Hunt, Morton and Hunt, Bernice. *The Divorce Experience*. New York: McGraw Hill. 1977.

Jung, Carl. *Psychological Reflections — A New Anthology of His Writings 1905-1961*. Jolande and Hull editors. New Jersey: Princeton University Press. 1970.

Kahn, Sandra S. *the Ex-wife Syndrome*. New York: Random House: 1990.

Krantzler, Mel. *Learning to Love Again*. New York: Thomas Y. Crowell. 1977.

Krantzler, Mel. *Creative Divorce*. New York: M. Evans and Co. 1973-1974.

Krantzler, Mel. *Creative Marriage*. New York: McGraw Hill. 1981.

Kreis, Bernadine. *To Love Again: An Answer to Loneliness*. New York: The Seabury Press. 1975.

Laing, R.D. *The Politics of the Family and Other Essays*. New York: Pantheon Books. 1971.

Landis, Judson T. and Mary G. *Building a Successful Marriage*. 5th edition. New Jersey: Prentice Hall. 1968.

Laswell, Marcia and Lobsenz, Norman M. *No Fault Marriage — The New Technique of Self-Counseling and What It Can Do To Help You*. New York: Doubleday. 1976.

LeShan, Eda. *Oh to Be 50 Again*. New York: Times Books, 1986.

List, Julie Autumn. *The Day the Loving Stopped*. New York: Seaview Books. 1980.

Lopas, Jeannette and R.R.. *Living in Step*. New York: Stein and Day. 1976.

Lopata, Helena Znaniecki. *Widowhood in an American City*. Cambridge, MA. 1973.

Maddox, Brenda. *The Half Parent*. New York: M. Evans and Co. 1975.

Mead, Margaret. *Male and Female.* New York: W.W. Norton. 1939.

Nirenberg, Jesse S. Ph.D. *Breaking Through to Each Other.* New York: Harper and Row. 1976.

Noble, June and William. *How to Live with Other People's Children.* New York: Hawthorne Books. 1977.

Pietropinto, Anthony, M.D. and Simenauer, Jacqueline. *Husbands and Wives, a Nationwide Survey of Marriage.* New York: Times Books. 1979.

Quinn, Jane Bryant. *Everyone's Money Book.* New York: Delta Publishing Co. 1978-1979.

Rogers, Carl. *On Personal Power, Inner Strength and Its Revolutionary Impact.* New York: Delacorte Press. 1977.

Roiphe, Anne. *Generation Without Memory.* Boston: Beacon Press. 1981.

Rosenbaum, Jean and Veryl. *Stepparenting.* Corte Madera, CA: Chander and Sharp Publishers, Inc.

Rosenbaum, Jean and Veryl. *Living with Teenagers.* New York: Stein and Day. 1980.

Rubin, Theodore Isaac, M.D. *Reconciliations: Inner Peace in an Age of Anxiety.* New York: Viking Press. 1980.

Russell, Bertrand. *History of Western Philosophy.* New York: Simon and Schuster/Touchstone. 1972.

Scarf, Maggie. *Unfinished Business.* New York: Doubleday. 1980.

Seifert, Anne. *His, Mine and Ours. A guide to keeping marriage from ruining a perfectly good relationship.* New York: MacMillan. 1979.

Shane, Dorlene V. and the United Survivors Health Cooperative. *Finance After Fifty, Financial Planning for the Rest of Your Life.* New York: Harper and Row. 1989.

Sheehy, Gail. *Pathfinders.* New York: Bantam Books. 1981.

Shilling, Dana with staff of John Hancock Financial Services. *Real Life, Real Answers.* New York: William Morris/Arbor House. 1988.

Spock, Benjamin. *Raising Children in a Difficult Time.* New York: W.W. Norton. 1974.

Spock, Benjamin S. and Morgan, Mary. M. *Spock on Spock.* New York: Pantheon Books. 1989.

Stewart, Marjabelle Young. *The New Etiquette Guide to Getting Married Again.* New York: St. Martin's Press. 1980.

Stuart, Irving R. and Abt, Laurence E., Editors. *Children of Separation and Divorce.* Grossman Publishers. 1972.

Sugarman, Daniel A., Ph.D. *Priceless Gifts: How to Give the Best to Those You Love.* New York: MacMillan. 1978.

Trafford, Abigail. *Crazy Time, Surviving Divorce.* New York: Harper and Row. 1982.

Vaillant, George. *Adaptaton to Life.* New York: Little Brown. 1977.

Wald, Esther. *The Remarried Family: Challenge and Promise.* New York: Family Service Association of America. 1981.

Wassmer, Arthur C., Ph.D. *Making Contact, a guide to overcoming shyness, making new relationships and keeping those you already have.* New York: Dial Press. 1978.

Weizman, Savine, G., Ph.D. and Kamm, Phyllis. *About Mourning, Support and Guidance for the Bereaved.* New York: Human Sciences Press. 1985.

Westoff, Leslie Aldridge. *The Second Time Around.* New York: Penguin Books. 1977.

Wolff, S. *Children Under Stress.* London: Allen Lane/ Penguin Press. 1969.

Newspapers and periodicals

Bakos, Susan Crain. Getting along with your child's other mother. *Cleveland Press* 9/13/81.

Begley, Sharon, with Clausen, Peggy. Does a contract help? *Newsweek* 1/10/83.

Bendetson, Jane. The caretakers. *New York Times Sunday Magazine* 2/10/91.

Berman, Claire. The instant parent. *Redbook* May 1981.

Brooks, Andrée. For stepfamilies: sharing and easing the tensions. *New York Times* 1/10/83.

Brooks, Andrée. Older singles found to value tradition. *New York Times* 6/5/83.

Brooks, Andrée. Becoming an "instant" step-mother. *New York Times* 8/4/86.

Broznan, Nadine. Less visible but heavier burdens as AIDS attacks people over 50. *New York Times* 11/26/90.

Budish, Armond D. Does marriage agreement pass four-part test? *Cleveland Press* 7/30/84.

Cimons, Marlene. AIDS cases up 29% for U.S. women. *Los Angeles Times* 11/30/90.

Collins, Glenn. Forgiving: a kind of freedom. *New York Times* 12/27/82.

Collins, Glenn. Some broken families retain many bonds. *New York Times* 12/20/82.

Collins, Glenn. Marriage is still popular. *New York Times* 6/18/87.

Curran, Dolores. What good families are doing right. *McCall's Magazine* March 1983.

Doudna, Christine. The weekend mother. *New York Times Magazine* 12/13/82.

Dullea, Georgia. *Holidays for a child of divorce. New York Times* 10/3/82.

Dullea, Georgie. Exploiters: they take, never give. *New York Times* 1/17/83.

Dullea, Georgia. The stepfamilies: new guides to live by. *New York Times* 1/4/79.

Getze, Linda Hubbard. Widowhood as a way of life. *Modern Maturity* June-July 1981.

Goleman, Daniel. Mortality study lends weight to patient's opinion. *New York Times* 3/21/91.

Harris, Ann P. Hers; discovering not all the world loves a middle-aged lover. *New York Times* 7/12/84.

Hinds, Michael de Courcy. *Discipline problems with a stepchild. New York Times* 3/23/81.

Leslie, Jacques. Stepping in. *New York Times Sunday Magazine* 4/15/84.

Levitan, Sar A. The U.S. family. *New York Times* 7/27/81.

"McCallmanack." Stepparents need legal clout. *McCall's Magazine* May 1990.

Peterson, Norma. Cry, baby! *American Way* March 1983.

Petterson, Karen S. In marriage game, odds similar for men and women. *U.S.A. Today* 12/20/90.

Rosen, Jan M. Your money; shielding children after remarriage. *New York Times* 9/22/90.

Rosen, Jan M. Your money; preserving assets of the old and ill. *New York Times* 3/23/91.

Rowland, Mary. 'Tis the season to get divorced. *New York Times* 1/13/91.

Shreve, Anita. Careers and the lure of motherhood. *New York Times Sunday Magazine* 11/21/82.

Slade, Margot. Siblings: war and peace. *New York Times Sunday Magazine* 3/11/84.

Sloane, Leonard. F.D.A. seeks labelling that would list effects of drugs on the elderly. *New York Times* 12/1/90.

Snyder, Pat and Bob. Second time around is not a replay. *The Plain Dealer* Cleveland 7/29/84.

White, Shelby. Signing a contract before marriage. *New York Times* 9/25/83.

Watch for these other titles in the
Mature Reader Series

HOW TO FIND A JOB
  When You're Over 50 — Don't Have a Resume —
  and Don't Know What to Look For!
If You're Over 50, YOU ARE THE TARGET
  How to avoid getting ripped off
TAKE A CAMEL TO LUNCH
  and Other Adventures for Mature Travelers
THE ENCYCLOPEDIA OF GRANDPARENTING
  Hundreds of Ideas to Entertain Your Grandchildren
DEALS AND DISCOUNTS
  If You're 50 or Older
I DARE YOU!
  How to Stay Young Forever
START YOUR OWN BUSINESS AFTER 50 – or 60 – or 70!
  64 People Who Did It Tell You How
THE BEGINNER'S ANCESTOR KIT
  For the Beginning Genealogist
THE NUTRITION GAME
  The Right Moves if You're Over 50
OVER 50 AND STILL COOKING!
  Recipes for Good Health and Long Life

Write for our free catalog.
Bristol Publishing Enterprises, Inc.
P.O. Box 1737
San Leandro, CA 94577